100
OLDTIME ROSES
FOR GARDENS
OF TODAY

100
OLDTIME ROSES
FOR GARDENS
OF TODAY

Allan A. Swenson

David McKay Company, Inc.
NEW YORK

Library of Congress Cataloging in Publication Data

Swenson, Allan A
100 oldtime roses for gardens of today.
Includes index.
1. Roses—Varieties. 2. Rose culture.   I. Title.
II. Title: Oldtime roses for gardens of today.
SB411.S98   635.9'33'372   79-13073
ISBN 0-679-51250-0

1 2 3 4 5 6 7 8 9 10
Manufactured in the United States of America

To: Dorothy Cannon Stemler, who touched so many lives through her love of the old and rare in rosedom. The beauty she saw and cultivated is today deeply rooted across America. Her dedication blooms in every old-fashioned rose that grows.

Acknowledgments

To all the helpful, considerate rose growers, veterans and novices alike, and the experts at rose gardens, nurseries, garden clubs, and rose societies, my grateful thanks for your help, advice, and encouragement. And with particular thanks and gratitude to Patricia Stemler Wiley, owner of Roses of Yesterday and Today, whose efforts through the years have so greatly encouraged many others to cultivate the best of the oldtime roses across America.

THE YEAR OF THE ROSE

1979

LOVE · FRIENDSHIP · PEACE

© AARS

For more than five thousand years, roses have been cultivated and admired by millions of people throughout the world. They have been living symbols of love, friendship, and peace. During the past few years, as roses have again climbed to new heights of popularity, there has been a concurrent rebirth of interest in oldtime roses. It is perhaps propitious that this book on oldtime roses should be published in 1979, designated as the "Year of the Rose" by horticultural organizations throughout America. May all roses bloom abundantly for years to come.

Contents

Introduction

Roses are deeply rooted in antiquity, and rightfully so. Few flowers have captured the admiration of so many millions of people through the eons of time. Today, spectacular roses of enormous blossom size, bushes profusely laden with glorious blooms, delicate miniatures, and delightful tree roses grace the gardens of America as they do gardens around the world.

Rose breeders have been a dedicated, innovative, and industrious group. From the genetic pool of roses, gathered from the farthest reaches of our globe, breeders have produced today's dazzling array of beautiful new roses. Every year, superb new varieties are created and tested, and their attributes compared with those developed and introduced just a few years ago. This important work and the combined efforts of hybridizers, rose growers, and the All-America Selection committee have contributed greatly to the wide range of roses we all enjoy today.

However, despite man's most ingenious efforts and best intentions, there are times when one cannot improve much on what has already been done. So it is with roses. Although new hybrid roses may bear larger blooms more abundantly, oldtime favorites still are in demand.

There has been, it seems, an accompanying phenomenon with flowers. Perhaps part of the reason for this revitalized appreciation of oldtime favorites can be traced to the attributes of these roses themselves. As well, more gardeners have been tracing the history and heritage of their own family's roots; perhaps this growing feeling of nostalgia has been partially responsible for the renewed interest in old-fashioned roses: As likely, according to many rose fanciers who have helped in preparing this book, the simple desire for more fragrant flowers is a major reason.

Other factors, of course, enter into this newfound feeling for oldtime roses. Some gardeners explain that they want roses that have just simple beauty. Others, more pragmatically, point to their desire to grow roses that are not as susceptible to diseases that afflict some of the more modern plants.

As more gardeners turn the fertile soil of their home grounds each year, planning to perfect their outdoor environment for lovelier living, old roses have emerged as new favorites. It is a good and welcome sign.

Assuming that those who search for these old-fashioned roses already are basically knowledgeable in rose care and culture, this book does not focus on rose growing itself, beyond a brief review of preferred rose-care practices. Instead, the focus is on those oldtime beauties that graced gardens from America's earliest years through our growing history to those that won popularity in the Roaring Twenties.

Roses, of course, date their fame much further back. Some trace their lineage to the Hanging Gardens of Babylon and ancient Persia, where nightingale songs filled the air that was scented with the aroma of damask roses.

Roses have been a part of national heritage and tradition in many countries through the centuries. The rose was the flower of the Greek goddess of love, Aphrodite, and of her Roman counterpart, Venus. In song and verse, roses have been the symbol of beauty and perfection from time immemorial. Egypt's fabeled empress Cleopatra seduced Marc Antony with the appealing scent of rose petals, according to legends of that time.

As the world entered the Christian era, white roses came to represent the Virgin Mary. The brier or moss rose is said to have sprung from the blood of Christ. In music, in painting, on tapestries and sculpture, roses have been favored symbols of beauty in many lands. Many ancient cathedrals have sparkling giant roses fashioned in their stained-glass windows.

As mankind has sought symbols to glorify events or mark special days, roses have found continuing favor. Historians believe that the Wars of the Roses started in a flower garden. During that lengthy conflict, Englishmen of York rallied beneath their white rose banner while those of Lancaster fought beneath their red rose flag.

Scholars, researching through the pages of history, believe the name "rose" was derived from the rose on the minted coins of Rhodes. Through the years, roses have flowered on banners and flags, and on such simple everyday things as coins and stamps.

With these glorious traditions, it is no wonder that old-fashioned roses are winning new admirers every day. My thanks to all those who have helped in the research for this book, who have given their enthusiastic encouragement and provided kind guidance; may your efforts bloom in gardens for many years to come.

—Allan A. Swenson
Windrows Farm
Kennebunk, Maine

1
A Whiff of Rose Heritage

Roses, like most flowers, have a long heritage. The fact is, all roses today are descended from wild roses found by plant collectors in many parts of the world. That may be difficult to believe, comparing a five-petaled old-fashioned rose with today's glorious modern hybrids, but these magnificent blooms are a real tribute to the talent of rose breeders through the years.

Many wild roses, however, do tend to bear double blooms, and some are especially noted for this characteristic. Even skilled amateur gardeners have been successful in planting wild roses that show an occasional double blossom and eventually producing descendants that consistently bear double blooms.

Since you have shown renewed interest in the oldtime favorites for your garden, perhaps a whiff of rose heritage will be useful.

The rose, fragrant as it is, has given its name to a large family, Rosaceae, of which it is the best-known member. There are more than a hundred genera in this family and as many as three thousand species. Some are bushes and shrubs, others vines, and a few are herbs. Related plants in the Rosaceae family include wild cherries and plums, crab apples, hawthorns, and many other commonly known plants. In America, wild roses have graced the mountains, plains, and deserts for centuries. These, of course, are related to other roses common in Europe and Asia. Generally speaking, roses, wherever found, are happiest and thrive best in temperate zones, including mountainous regions from India and Mexico to China and Russia.

Many experts believe the rose was the first flower to be brought into cultivation. There is little doubt that roses have captured the imagination and affection of gardeners throughout the centuries. They were grown in ancient Babylon and Greece. Old Roman records tell of roses growing profusely in gardens throughout the Roman Empire. There are many mentions of roses in ancient Chinese literature as well. Roses were loved and poems written about their beauty and fragrance as early as A.D. 1000 in China. Rose petals as well as blooms were used lavishly in those early days of budding civilizations. The Moors brought roses from Syria across Europe to Spain, rooting there the first yellow roses to be seen in Europe.

During the Middle Ages, roses were cultivated for medicinal value; they are still used in perfume industries in Asia and Europe today. With our renewed interest in natural foods, rose hips again have attracted attention, having such high vitamin C content that they far surpass citrus juices, in this valuable vitamin content. Rose hip teas, jams, preserves are high on the list of favored natural foods today.

Sniffing back through the pages of rose history, we can determine that one of the first roses to be cultivated and domesticated was the double cabbage rose, *R. centifolia*, which originated in the Caucasus Mountains. These giant pink roses grow wild there to this day. Cabbage roses were transplanted to ancient Greece and Rome, and in later days the French gave this rose the name Provence rose.

The distinctly scented damask rose, *R. damascena*, was introduced centuries ago from Asia Minor. Another common forebear of modern roses, and old-fashioned ones as well, is the French rose, *R. gallica*. This originated in Europe and western Asia. These three types are the major parent stock for today's roses, many oldtime favorites still resembling them in size, profusion of bloom, and growing habit.

Through the years, as rosarians have traveled the globe to seek out other unusual and attractive new plants for domestication and use in plant-breeding programs, Chinese species have contributed to rose heritage. Three in particular—the China or monthly rose, *R. chinensis;* the climbing Cathay rose, *R. cathayensis;* and the tea rose, *R. odorata*—have added their distinctive characteristics to rose heritage.

There are other progenitors, of course. The Austrian brier, *R. foetida*—actually from Asia—with its deep yellow color; the sturdy rugosa rose, *R. rugosa*, of China, Korea, and Japan; and two Japanese species, *R. multiflora and R. wichuraiana*, also have been incorporated in rose breeding.

From Europe, the Scotch rose, *R. spinosissima*, and the sweetbrier, *R. eglanteria;* and from North America, the pasture rose, *R. carolina*, the climbing prairie rose, *R. setigera*, and the California rose, *R. california*, are rooted in rose culture history.

Knowing something about the original parentage, sometimes dating back centuries, will enable you to understand how the characteristics of different types of roses have contributed to the old-fashioned roses of today, as well as the more modern ones. For example, Father Hugo's rose, *R. hugonis*, is from China. It is a graceful shrub with arching branches that are covered with pale yellow, single flowers. It is perhaps the earliest rose to bloom. From its study stock, many others have been developed. Harison's yellow rose, *R. harisonii*, is a hybrid between the Scotch rose and the Austrian brier. This nearly pest-free shrub with lovely semidouble (between single and full double) flowers blooms a rich, butter-yellow color.

In this book, you'll find descriptions of many oldtime roses available for your growing pleasure. They have been divided into different classes according to their growth and blooming habits, from perpetuals to climbing roses. Knowing about their lineage can perhaps help you select those that will best suit your rose gardening plans.

The hybrid perpetual class reached its popularity toward the end of the last century. These roses were especially favored for their hardiness and strong, sturdy growth. In most cases, perpetual roses were noted as well for their rich fragrance and great bursts of blooms in summer, plus, of course, the continuation of flowers.

Cabbage roses with typically giant pink blooms, *R. centifolia*, native to the Caucasus area, have been responsible for imparting large bloom size and fine fragrance to many versions and hybrids you can grow today.

Another highly fragrant ancient rose, the rose-pink damask rose, *R. damascena*, is actually a native of the area that was ancient Babylon. It too gave its desired characteristics, especially its aroma, to many other hybrids through the years.

Moss roses with their mossy buds and stalks appeared as a natural sport or mutant of the cabbage rose about 1596. To this day, the distinctive mossy look and feel of these roses continues, according to rosarians.

The earliest roses brought into cultivation from around the world typically had one annual blooming period. The damask roses, however, occasionally bloomed again in the fall. This tendency, of course, was preferred by many gardeners and rose admirers, and eventually was bred into other roses over the years.

China roses, *R. chinensis*, are native to the Orient and were first introduced to Europe in the late 1700s. These too bloomed several times, and in warmer climates often bloomed monthly. This ever-blooming habit earned them great popularity and was blended into new roses with other desired characteristics to yield the early old-fashioned roses that are still popular today. With careful selection and breeding, the most desired characteristics of both parents can be produced in the offspring.

According to reputable rosarians, polyantha roses are usually very low shrubs, almost everblooming, that produce large clusters of small but seldom fragrant flowers.

Rugosa roses are classically simple and, with proper breeding, produce exceptional hedge plants with thorny canes bearing thick, wrinkled foliage and large, fragrant, and loosely formed flowers.

Most of the climbing roses are hybrids of·*R. multiflora* and *R. wichuraiana*, somewhere in their well-rooted heritage.

The continued cross breeding has yielded climbing forms of hybrid teas and hybrid perpetuals. Rose breeders have been, it would seem, a marvelously creative lot.

Background of the newer shrub roses dates to the Penzance sweet-briers, hybrids of *R. elganteria*, and the Pemberton roses, hybrids of the musk rose, *R. moschata*.

In about 1810, the tea rose, *R. odorata*, was transplanted from

China. This remontant or repeating bloomer also found fast friends.

Perhaps a short review and description of old roses that are the original parents of today's popular old-fashioned roses would be appropriate.

The Scotch rose, *R. spinosissima*, is a low bush, densely covered with slender prickles. It produces white and pale pink or even yellowish flowers about one and one-half to two inches across.

The sweetbrier or eglantine rose, *R. eglanteria*, is a stiff, erect, branching bush. It bears pink blooms and also has sweet-smelling foliage.

The so-called dog rose, *R. canina*, includes many subspecies and varieties. It is common along the hedgerows and byways of England and bears pinkish to white single flowers, one to two inches across.

A large fruited apple rose, *R. pomifera*, has long been prized for its large, scarlet rose hips. These may mature an inch or more across.

Dating from olden days, the parent of the Ayrshire rose, *R. arvensis*, is a very thorny shrub, with decumbent or creeping branches.

The French rose, *R. gallica*, has been popular for eons. It is a small shrub, three to four feet high, and has been cultivated and bred for its familiar scent for hundreds of years.

The damask rose, *R. damascena*, is similar to the French rose; however, it is larger and has the typically damask rose smell.

The cabbage rose, *R. centifolia*, dates its heritage to ancient times and has remained popular for its double, fragrant flowers. These two favored characteristics have led to its use in breeding of improved newer varieties through the years.

The cinnamon rose, *R. cinnamomea*, is a familiar, hardy, old garden species. It still can be found along fences and roadsides and is popular for its double, fragrant flowers in shades of red with blooms two inches or more across.

There are, of course, many wild North American roses. Among them, these are the most common:

The prickly rose, *R. acicularis*, has spiny stems and leaves composed of from five to nine leaflets. It grows wild from Quebec to Alaska and south to mid-America.

The pasture rose, *R. virginiana*, grows from a few feet to six feet tall. It bears a few flowers, two to three inches across and sometimes double. In the wild it occurs from Newfoundland to Wisconsin and south to Georgia, one of the most common wild roses of the eastern United States.

The prairie rose, *R. setigera*, is a large shrub with a tendency to climb. Its leaves usually have three leaflets and it bears rose-pink flowers that whiten with age. A handsome rose, it grows wild from Ontario to Wisconsin and as far south as Florida and Texas.

The California rose, *R. california*, is a sparsely prickled shrub that matures three to nine feet tall. It flowers nearly year round and is most common in marshy or moist areas along streams, where it may grow as a thicket in warmer climates.

Although there are numerous wild roses across America, most of the parentage of cultivated domesticated garden roses stems from Europe and China. Actually, Asiatic roses are the key stock of today's roses.

The tea rose, *R. odorata* from western China, has the happy habit of blooming more or less continuously through the year in appropriate climates. Its five to seven leaflets, typically tea-rose blooms, and fragrant, tea-scented flowers are from one to three inches across in white, pink, or salmon yellow.

Also from China, the China or Bengal rose, *R. chinensis*, is rather similar to *R. odorata*, but the plants are smaller and the flowers are almost odorless.

The Austrian brier rose, *R. foetida*, a three- to five-foot shrub, has typically deep yellow flowers, two to three inches in diameter. Its influence in oldtime breeding can be seen today with the yellow hues in many roses.

From the Orient also, multiflora roses, *R. multiflora*, are attractive shrubs with long, arching branches. Flowers are tiny, usually one-half to less than one inch across, but are borne in dense panicles of twenty-five to a hundred.

The memorial rose, *R. wichuraiana*, with its long, nearly prostrate stems and glossy foliage, is clearly another progenitor of many roses. It bears clusters of slightly fragrant blooms, about an inch across.

Rugosa roses have lent some of their characteristics to other roses too. The rugosa or wrinkled foliage and large, conspicuous red, pink or white flowers are well known. The hips too are conspicuously large.

Another yellow progenitor, *R. hugonis*, is a handsome and hardy shrub. It produces an abundance of light yellow blooms early in spring, an obvious advantage in a breeding stock.

There are, of course, many other original wild roses that have been collected from the far corners of the earth. These too have served in breeding programs over the years, which have led to the thousands of roses that grace gardens today. Rosarians explain that the present-day old-fashioned roses, as well as the modern rose varieties, are primarily based on these key originals: *R. centifolia*, *R. chinensis*, *R. damascena*, *R. foetida*, *R. gallica*, and *R. odorata*. The valued traits of continuous blooming and fragrances can be attributed mainly to the influence of *R. chinensis* and *R. odorata*. The yellows that occur in coloration of many roses are most likely the influence of *R. foetida*.

The parenthood of *R. gallica*, *R. damascena*, and *R. centifolia* has contributed hardiness and vigor, as well as scent and desired flower size and color. In producing the climbing and rambler types, *R. multiflora* and *R. wichuraiana* have no doubt played a vital part.

The study of rose history, like the tracing of one's own family roots, can be a complex and difficult task. This chapter is not meant to be a complete review of the roots of roses through the centuries. It is, however, perhaps helpful to know some of the background and genesis of old-fashioned roses and how their progenitors have led to the continuing wealth of modern roses that grace gardens throughout America and the world today.

2
100 All-Time Oldtime Favorites Available Today

There are native species of roses in practically every region of the world. Just which one was the first cultivated rose and where it appeared, nobody can say with certainty.

Perhaps the best way to underscore the continual development of roses is to return to the earliest known botanical facts. Originally, all of our roses came from species roses. If you cross species roses, you get a new hybrid type of rose. When you cross this new type, you create another new type. There are types and classifications of roses, just as there are races of people and breeds of dogs and types within the races and breeds of all living things.

If you remember the "begats" in the Book of Genesis in the Holy Bible, you have a famous example of how people have descended from their ancestors. The history of roses follows similar lines.

It is believed by rosarians and botanists that Rosa Gallica is perhaps the Adam of roses that are native to the Western Hemisphere. When Rosa Gallica was crossed with Rosa Moschata, the result was the Autumn Damask. Rosa Gallica, when crossed with Rosa Canina, begat the Alba; and when crossed with Rosa Phoenicia, begat the Damask. The Damask, crossed with Alba, begat Centifolia, and so on, and so on.

In the late 1700s, botanists discovered everblooming roses in the gardens of the subtropics in China. Because of their tealike fragrance, those roses became known as tea roses.

When the Chinese tea rose was crossed with Gallica descendants, the first result was the Bourbon. Bourbon roses crossed with a Tea begat Hybrid Perpetual. Those crossed back to tea roses produced Hybrid Tea, and so on, begat after begat. Modern rose growers are, of course, studiously at work on more begats. It is estimated that roses have been growing for thirty-five million years. A fossilized rose, unearthed at Crooked River, Oregon, was examined by scientists. These learned men claim that the fossilized rose may have existed back in the Cretaceous Age, seventy million years ago.

When you begin to plant your garden of oldtime roses, you can be assured that their roots trace back through more begats than you realized. Roses indeed are one of the most popular flowers known to mankind through the ages.

In this chapter you'll find roses grouped according to their blooming or growing habits.

If you are mathematically inclined, you may notice that when you add up all the categories you get not 100 oldtime roses but 104.

First comes a straight alphabetical listing of the roses in the various categories.

Then comes a thumbnail description of each rose. Many of these descriptions are illustrated with photographs of the roses in bloom.

The "Perpetual" category includes roses that are repeat bloomers, roses that yield beauty all season. Next is the "Climbing" category. Then come the "Annual" roses, types that bloom once a year. And finally is a group of "Other Desirable Oldtime Roses," ranging from hybrid tea to polyantha roses.

All photos in this chapter are courtesy of Roses of Yesterday and Today, Watsonville, California.

OLDTIME ROSES DESCRIBED IN THIS CHAPTER

Perpetual Oldtime Roses: The Repeat Bloomers

Alfred de Dalmas
American Beauty
Arrillaga
Autumn Delight
Baroness Rothschild
Baron Giron de l'Ain
Baronne Prevost
Belle Poitevine
Bishop Darlington
Blanc Double de Coubert
Candeur Lyonnaise
Catherine Mermet
Comte de Chambord
Delicata
Deuil de Paul Fontaine
Everest
Ferdinand Pichard
Frau Dagmar Hastrup

Frau Karl Druschki
Gabriel Noyelle
General Jacqueminot
Georg Arends
Green Rose
Gruss an Teplitz
Heinrich Munch
Henry Nevard
Jacques Cartier
Kathleen
La Reine Victoria
Lissy Horstmann
Mabel Morrison
Madame Ernest Calvat
Madame Isaac Pereire
Madame Louis Leveque
Madame Pierre Oger
Maman Cochet

Marchioness of Londonderry
Marchioness of Lorne
May Queen
Mermaid
Mrs. John Laing
Nastarana
Paul Neyron
Pax
Penelope
Prince Camille de Rohan
Reine des Violettes
Roger Lambelin
Rosa Damascena Bifera

Rosa de Rescht
Rosa Paulii
Rosa Rugosa Rubra
Rose du Roi
Roseraie de l'Hay
Rosette Delizy
Rubrifolia
Rugosa Magnifica
Ruskin
Safrano
Salet
Sombreuil
Souvenir de la Malmaison

Oldtime Climbing Roses

Climbing American Beauty
Climbing Cecile Bruner
Climbing Columbia
Climbing Lady Forteviot

Climbing La France
Climbing Shot Silk
Felicite et Perpetue

Annual Oldtime Roses

Agnes
Austrian Copper
Belle de Crecy
Belle of Portugal
Camaieux
Centifolia Muscosa Alba
Charles de Mills
Common Moss
De Meaux

Dupontii
Eglantine
Fantin-Latour
Father Hugo's Rose (Hugonis)
Felicite Parmentier
Koenigin von Daenemarck
Lawrence Johnston
Madame Hardy
Maiden's Blush

Petite de Hollande
Rosa Damascena Trigintipetala
Striped Moss

Tuscany Superb
Variegata di Bologna

Other Desirable Oldtime Roses

Dainty Bess
Gruss an Aachen
Gruss an Coburg
La France
Madame Butterfly
Margaret Ann Baxter

Marytje Cazant
Ophelia
Orange Triumph
Perle d'Or
Souvenir de Madame Boullet
White Pet

Perpetual Oldtime Roses: The Repeat Bloomers

Alfred de Dalmas

This hybrid moss rose dates to 1855, and grows 2 to 3 feet tall. It flowers repeatedly, providing profusions of blooms over the growing season.

This rose is a hardy, compact, and low-growing type which blooms much like a floribunda. Its bushy growth makes it especially suitable for low hedges bordering other garden areas.

Small, nicely mossed buds open to become dainty flowers, which range from white to a blush pink in color. Its other popular name is Mousseline.

American Beauty

This hybrid perpetual rose origi-nated about 1875 and grows 4 to 5 feet tall. It flowers repeatedly, bearing pink to shaded, smoky carmine blooms. Do not be misled by its name. The so-called American Beauty rose sold in florist shops bears no real relationship or resemblance to this rose.

American Beauty of 1875 vintage was a popular rose of the Gay Nineties, most likely for its ability to bloom again and again. Among old-fashioned roses, this should please nostalgia buffs as well as anyone desiring a profusely and repeatedly blooming old favorite.

Arrillaga

This hybrid perpetual, circa 1929, grows 5 to 7 feet tall and flowers repeatedly. When it blooms, the flowers, only two-thirds open, are often as big as medium-size cabbages. The rich tone of pale pink is a welcome sight, and the fragrance is elegant.

For large blooms among old-fashioned roses, Arrillaga has flowers that are bigger and more striking than many modern hybrid tea roses.

Autumn Delight

This hybrid musk rose, developed

in 1933, has a repeat flowering habit and will grow 5 to 6 feet tall.

The soft white, almost single flowers are 3 to 4 inches across with prominent stamens. Blooms are borne in large clusters on a sturdy plant that serves well as a specimen to stand alone, against a wall or fence, or in groups as a decorative hedge. Autumn Delight provides an abundance of blooms and is rated superior by fanciers of old-style roses.

Baroness Rothschild

This hybrid perpetual, which traces its ancestry back to 1868, grows 4 to 5 feet tall and is another that flowers repeatedly.

Back in 1869, Baroness Rothschild, for whom it was named, wrote that in her opinion it was the rose of the year. This distinct, large, very double rose has cupped, fragrant, clear pink blooms which are borne in profusion. An additional advantage is that Baroness Rothschild offers good cutting stems for use as indoor bouquets and displays.

Baron Giron de l'Ain

Dating from 1897, this hybrid perpetual flowers repeatedly on plants 3 to 4 feet high.

Its unique blooms have found wide popularity. Their color is ruby red, but the petals are edged with white, a nicely defined contrast. The plants are healthy and have an upright growing habit with large, medium green foliage. Flowers are about 3 inches across and classically cupped with the added appeal of intense old-rose fragrance. There are few thorns on this rose.

Baronne Prevost

A hybrid perpetual, circa 1839, this 4 to 5 foot tall rose flowers repeatedly in home gardens.

Baronne Prevost is one of the many hybrid perpetuals that was grown and named in the mid 1800s and is one of the earliest, finest, and most prolific. With the classic form of the old roses, it produces big, flat, open flowers with many small, tightly packed rose-pink petals that are silvery on the reverse side and richly perfumed.

This desirable rose is one of the first hybrid perpetuals to bloom and it continues its profusion of flowers until frost. You can count on it for strong, healthy growth as a hardy, compact, lovely plant.

Belle Poitevine

This rugosa from 1894 flowers repeatedly on 4 to 8 foot tall plants. According to its adherents, few roses, if any, excel this one for garden beauty and ornamentation. It is extremely hardy and resists rose pests, needs no pruning except to remove deadwood, and thrives for years. You must, of course, prune to desired size and shape.

Belle Poitevine will produce double lilac pink blooms 4 inches across with a compelling fragrance that attracts bees well. It produces many edible hips with high vitamin C content, and these produce fragrant, tasty tea.

Bishop Darlington

A hybrid musk of 1926 vintage, this 4 to 7 foot rose flowers repeatedly and beautifully.

Its slender buds of coral color open to 3-inch-wide semidouble flowers in shades ranging from ivory to peach pink. An upright plant, it serves well as background for low-growing plants. Reported to be sturdy and to bloom profusely in summer's heat, it also holds its blooming habit well into early fall.

Blanc Double de Coubert

A rugosa dating to 1892, this repeatedly blooming rose grows 3 to 5 feet tall.

Considered by many to be among the best of the few white rugosas in existence, Blanc Double de Coubert has handsome, typically rugosa foliage and is hardy anywhere. During the season, large, pure white, fairly double flowers grow profusely in cycle after cycle. They are followed by glowing red rose hips which are plentiful in vitamin C for jam and jelly.

Candeur Lyonnaise

Among hybrid perpetuals, this 4 to 5 foot rose is one of the exceptional white types that flower repeatedly. Beginning in early spring and continuing to the first hard frost, Candeur Lyonnaise is literally covered with 5-inch blooms that have delightful, lightly fringed petals. A striking specimen that stirs interest and captures attention, this profusely blooming hybrid perpetual also serves well as a cut flower for indoor displays.

Catherine Mermet

Developed in 1869, this tea rose

performs well, flowering repeatedly on a 3 to 4 foot plant.

The strikingly long, pointed, flesh-pink buds develop into large, double, open flowers. Although this lovely tea is among the best of the old tea roses, perfuming the garden air with its aroma, it is best grown where winters are mild.

Comte de Chambord

Dating from 1860, this 4 foot tall rose flowers repeatedly.

Exquisite buds of many tightly formed petals open gradually to a flat flower of rich pink, edged with petals that are reflexed (flexing outward) and tinged lightly with lilac. This rose grows as a compact plant with light-green foliage, and its lovely flowers are intensely perfumed. One of the best for an old-fashioned garden, according to its admirers.

Delicata

Everest

This rugosa rose, from 1898, flowers repeatedly on bushes 3 to 4 feet tall.

Among rugosas, these are extremely hardy and disease resistant, and bear beautiful as well as fragrant blooms. The large rose hips with their typically high vitamin C content are a colorful and nutritious addition.

Delicata has large, semidouble, lilac pink flowers borne on short stems. The foliage is mintlike with a fascinating fragrance. You will discover that this rose produces flowers and hips at the same time, and when fully matured, the hips may be the size of small crab apples.

Deuil de Paul Fontaine

This hybrid moss rose grows 2 to 4 feet tall, flowers repeatedly, and dates its heritage to 1873.

Plants have dark-green foliage, and canes are decoratively covered with red thorns and bristles. The big blooms are bold and striking tones of crimson, black, purple, and brown red. For those who prefer deeply colored roses, there are few that can compare with Deuil de Paul Fontaine's bold, dark coloration.

A hybrid perpetual dating to 1927, this rose flowers repeatedly on a plant 5 to 6 feet tall.

Many rosarians favor it for its 5 to 6 inch blooms and refer to it as the king of white roses. The bush itself and the giant, fragrant white flowers are striking as a specimen in gardens. This excellent hybrid perpetual thrives when well fed and watered heavily to encourage its continuous, robust performance.

Ferdinand Pichard

This hybrid perpetual from about 1927 grows 5 to 6 feet tall and flowers repeatedly.

Petals of the fragrant Ferdinand Pichard are cupped and crisp in appearance. The double flowers are striped red and pale pink, or sometimes white. This unique coloration provides lovely displays. Foliage itself is almost lettuce green, so you will find that the contrast of foliage and blooms is especially pleasing. It responds particularly well to training, or you can grow it in a low, spreading form if you wish.

This rugosa rose from 1914 grows 2 ½ to 3 feet tall and flowers repeatedly.

A five-petaled type of oldtime rose, its three-inch blooms with satiny petals have clear pink color. Admirers say that these blossoms appear like pink stars in the attractive rugosa foliage of the plant. Following petal fall, the large red rose hips add their own striking color to the plant. Frau Dagmar Hastrup blooms are extremely fragrant.

Frau Karl Druschki

Another wonderful white hybrid perpetual, circa 1900, Frau Karl Druschki flowers repeatedly on plants 4 to 6 feet tall.

This rose is also called Snow Queen because of the brilliant white of its blooms. With strong canes and branches, it has many blooms and buds continually on what many call the most queenly of hybrid perpetual roses.

A hybrid moss rose of 1933 vintage, this delightful rose flowers repeatedly on bushes 4 to 6 feet tall.

The well-mossed buds and partially open flowers are flesh pink ranging to salmon, but when open to semidouble flowers they also provide cream tones with yellow coloration at the base of the petals. The canes háve an arching growth habit that in southern areas makes the plant useful as a climber. Rosarians note that this is a cross of Salet with a deep hybrid tea rose. You may train this rose to a smaller growth pattern by shortening its canes, since it blooms repeatedly.

General Jacqueminot

A hybrid perpetual that dates to 1853, this fine old rose flowers repeatedly on plants 4 to 5 feet tall.

Among rose fanciers, General Jacqueminot, or briefly, General Jack, is widely acclaimed as one of the most sweetly scented roses. The soft, smooth, velvety petals have their own special grace and the vivid crimson color is a joy to see. This is one of the most appealing of oldtime roses for today.

Georg Arends

A hybrid perpetual from 1910 that grows 5 to 6 feet tall, this rose flowers repeatedly.

You will find its long, sleek buds are a satiny pink and open to display the same lustrous pink color throughout the bloom. A beauty in the garden, the unique satiny crinkles of its petals make this a delight for cut displays indoors. Fortunately, it is both fragrant and long lasting as a cut flower.

Green Rose

From eons ago, *Rosa chinensis viridiflora* was introduced generally in 1856 and flowers repeatedly on plants 4 to 5 feet tall.

One of the oddities of the rose world, the Green Rose is more a novelty than an attractive and striking plant. The flowers seem not to be flowers at all, but rather a unique freak of foliage. The greenish buds open to reveal double leaf-green, flowerlike displays edged with bronze. Although not an especially appealing plant, it has its value for its uniqueness and can be used for interesting flower arrangements with other roses.

Gruss an Teplitz

A hybrid China rose circa 1897, this flowers repeatedly on compact 3 to 4 foot plants.

According to rosarians, Gruss an Teplitz has ancestors that trace to one Bourbon rose, two China roses, and one tea rose. A nicely spreading plant that can be used where low-growing roses are desired, it has medium-sized double blooms in a dusky red tone. Its fragrance is almost spicy.

Heinrich Munch

This hybrid perpetual, circa 1911, flowers repeatedly on 4 to 5 foot tall plants.

Among the so-called cabbage roses, Heinrich Munch has blossoms that are especially large, often measuring 7 or more inches across when fully opened. The blooms are soft, delicate pink, and especially full of petals. The aroma is heady and more powerful than many other roses, which also makes this a favorite among oldtime-rose enthusiasts.

Henry Nevard

This hybrid perpetual from 1924 grows 4 to 5 feet high and flowers repeatedly.

Henry Nevard has leathery, dark green foliage and produces large, strikingly double, dark red flowers that are lovely in both shape and form. It is richly perfumed and grows successfully from Arizona to Canada, where it has won just acclaim from many home gardeners.

Jacques Cartier

This Portland rose from 1868 grows 2 to 3½ feet tall and flowers repeatedly on a nicely compact plant.

Clear pink 3-inch flowers with intense fragrance are borne in abundance. The many petals create an appearance of fluffy bloom. This plant has closely spaced, light green foliage that encircles its blooms. You can enjoy Jacques Cartier in low borders. Their growth and bloom seem close to the autumn damask roses; this is an excellent one for long-lasting bouquets.

Kathleen

A hybrid musk rose from about 1922, this flowers repeatedly on 6 to 15 foot tall plants.

Kathleen is vigorous and healthy with notably disease-resistant foliage. It bears large clusters of tiny, pointed China pink buds that open to 1½-inch single white flowers with stiff yellow stamens. These resemble apple blossoms and are so strongly perfumed they readily attract many bees.

This musk rose produces clusters of orange rose hips. Rosarians note that it grows well in filtered as well as full sun.

La Reine Victoria

This Bourbon rose of 1872 grows 4 to 6 feet high and flowers repeatedly.

Bearing cupped, rosy pink blooms with shades to deeper rose on its outer petals, La Reine Victoria has won many admirers. It is intensely fragrant and lasts well both in the garden and as a cut flower for bouquets. This has remained one of the all-time old rose favorites.

Lissy Horstmann

This hybrid tea rose is a somewhat more modern rose dating to about 1940 and grows 2 to 3 feet tall. Reputedly it existed somewhat earlier.

This large, double scarlet crimson rose is strongly perfumed. Created in Germany, it has long, strong stems and its blooms are nicely cupped. For those who prefer large, soundly red roses, Lissy Horstmann is a good choice.

Mabel Morrison

This hybrid perpetual, circa 1878, flowers repeatedly on 3 to 4 foot tall plants.

Noted for its blue-green foliage and surprisingly low, compact growth, Mabel Morrison does well in beds and borders. The blooms are profuse and highly fragrant. Flowers are white with a blush of palest pink at times and have up to 30 petals in a delightful and delicate cupped shape.

Madame Ernest Calvat

A Bourbon rose, circa 1888, this flowers repeatedly on a 5 to 7 foot tall plant.

Reportedly originated as a sport of Madame Isaac Pereire, this has large, cupped, and quartered blooms with many rich pink petals. These curl and whirl in an attractive manner. This rose is one of those with intense fragrance. Growers report that some bushes may revert a cane or two back to Madame Isaac Pereire, but that is not common. When it happens, you will have rose-madder blooms and swirled pink petaled ones on the same plant, a fascinating oddity.

Madame Isaac Pereire

This Bourbon rose, circa 1880, flowers repeatedly on 4 to 6 foot plants.

As a fine shrub rose, Madame Isaac Pereire has the reputation of being perhaps the most powerfully fragrant of all roses. Its scent seems to fill the entire garden. Flowers are large, intense rose-madder and shaded magenta. The rolled petals open to great blooms among its bold, big foliage. Many experts and home gardeners alike have been strongly attracted to this fragrant, lovely rose for specimen planting.

Madame Louis Leveque

A hybrid moss from 1874, this

flowers repeatedly on 4 to 5 foot tall plants.

Madame Louis Leveque grows as an upright plant with bright green, long, pointed leaves. It bears large double cupped flowers of soft lilac pink which are very fragrant among large roses. In addition to their attractive, subtle color, the blooms are large, making this variety excellent for garden displays.

Madame Pierre Oger

Another Bourbon rose, dating to 1878, this grows 5 to 6 feet tall and flowers repeatedly.

According to rose lore, this sprouted as a sport of La Reine Victoria. It grows well as an erect plant with smooth, light green foliage, and continually produces new flowering shoots. The blooms are creamy flesh color and have a rosy blush. Like its parent, this rose is fragrantly perfumed.

Maman Cochet

A delightful old tea rose from

1893, this flowers repeatedly on a 3 to 4 foot sturdy plant.

One of the greatly admired oldtime tea roses, Maman Cochet bears blooms up to 4 inches across, which are beautifully double formed and intensely scented. Flowers are cream, often shaded with pale pink or other tones of rose and even at times chestnut red. This varying depth of color is a common characteristic of tea roses. You can enjoy this rose outdoors or as a cut flower from bud through opening.

Marchioness of Londonderry

A hybrid perpetual dating to 1893, this flowers repeatedly on 5 to 7 foot tall plants.

An extraordinary rose of enormous size and many petals, Marchioness of Londonderry has delicate cream and pale flesh tones that blend beautifully. Among oldtime roses, this has won many adherents as their favorite for its sturdy growth, large plant and bloom size, and responsiveness to fertilizing for exceptional performance. It also is, happily, a fragrant rose.

Marchioness of Lorne

Another repeatedly flowering hybrid perpetual, this dates to 1889 and grows on a 4 to 5 foot plant.

It was among many beautiful roses created by William Paul, a noted British rose producer in the mid-nineteenth century. It is sturdy, responds to pegging or training in an arched position, and produces hundreds of flowers every season. Blooms are rich, almost glowing deep rose, double in form, and fragrant.

May Queen

Dating from about 1898, this hybrid *R. wichuraiana* flowers repeatedly on enormous plants up to 25 feet in height.

Perfectly designed for walls and fences, it grows rapidly. Glossy foliage is disease resistant and hardier than many other large-flowered climbing roses. May Queen produces many dusky pink, cupped, double flowers that have a fruity fragrance.

Mermaid

This 1918 hybrid bracteata grows 15 to 25 feet and flowers repeatedly.

A rapidly growing climbing plant, Mermaid performs well on fences and expanses of buildings or at property borders. It is resistant to black spot disease. The small, tight buds open into large soft yellow—sometimes pale yellow—blooms up to 6 inches across. These flowers are single with nicely prominent gold stamens. Many gardeners like the fact that this rose drops spent petals and remains clean looking, with buds and new flowers opening regularly. It does best in southern areas.

Mrs. John Laing

Dating back to 1887, this hybrid perpetual flowers repeatedly in many gardens on 5 to 6 foot plants.

This is one of the more popular large, pink, and highly fragrant perpetual roses. It has noted winter hardiness as well as profuse and continuing blooming habit.

Home gardeners have marveled that Mrs. John Laing plants can be covered with buds and flowers, producing glorious displays, for many weeks.

Nastarana

This *R. moschata*, developed in 1879, flowers repeatedly on 3 to 4 foot plants.

According to rosarians, the slender, upright plant with its tiny, light green leaves actually emerged from a cross between *Rosa moschata* and *Rosa chinensis*. It bears clusters of 10 to 25 semidouble, pure white flowers, 2 inches across. The pale pink buds are exceedingly fragrant. You can use this in small, low plantings for its delicate foliage and flower forms.

Paul Neyron

A hybrid perpetual, circa 1869, this flowers repeatedly on 5 to 6 foot plants.

One of its noted characteristics is the hundreds of tight petals on the enormous blooms, which may exceed 6 to 7 inches across. The blooms are rose pink, handsomely large, and fragrant.

Pax

This hybrid musk rose from 1918 flowers repeatedly on large 6 to 8 foot plants.

The shiny, healthy-looking foliage grows in a graceful pattern, making this rose useful on fences, or along stone walls. Flowers are 4 to 5 inches across, creamy white, and almost single, with a fragrance typical of all hybrid musk roses. It is in short supply unfortunately.

Penelope

A hybrid musk from 1924, this flowers repeatedly on 5 to 8 foot tall plants.

This is a versatile rose with glossy, attractive foliage, salmon buds that open to reveal creamy white to pale pink blooms. The flower clusters of 2½ to 3 inch blooms, and the buds as well, have a musky fragrance. In the fall, the forming hips are uniquely apple green in color and change gradually to a coral pink.

Prince Camille de Rohan

A hybrid perpetual circa 1861, this flowers repeatedly on plants 5 to 6 feet tall.

These strong, hardy plants are enduring and handsome. The richly perfumed blooms are dark red with an almost velvety texture. Flowers are large and full-bodied blooms of deep velvety crimson.

Reine des Violettes

This hybrid perpetual rose from 1870 grows 6 to 8 feet tall and flowers repeatedly.

The hardy, thornless, and glossy-leaved shrub stands proudly. Flowers are many petaled and fragrant. The blooms themselves range from pink through lilac and blue tones to deep magenta and blend into a smoky blue color effect. It perhaps is the bluest of any rose, including modern ones, and foliage is peppery scented.

Roger Lambelin

This hybrid perpetual from 1890 stands 4 to 6 feet tall and flowers repeatedly.

For best results this variety prefers lots of food and water. It will stand sleekly tall and produce handsome crimson purple flowers, the petals edged with white. This truly different rose offers the opportunity for growing a striking specimen in your garden.

Rosa Damascena Bifera

This classic autumn damask rose of ancient times matures to 3 to 4 feet and flowers repeatedly.

Historians and poets alike have extolled its virtues from Greek and Roman days. The Spanish brought this rose to the new world and called it Castilian or Rose of Castile. Clusters of several dainty pink buds with long graceful sepals open one after the other to reveal 3½ inch very double flowers. The foliage is light yellowish green, brushed with gray. This ancient rose deserves a place in every oldtime garden to preserve its distinctive place in rose history. The intense damask perfume from cut bouquets fills a room.

Rosa de Rescht

This autumn damask rose grows 2 to 3 feet tall and flowers repeatedly.

From its heritage in Persia and England, this compact plant has endured for many years. Leaves are closely spaced on canes up to the flowers and seem to encircle the blooms. The 2 to 2½ inch rosette blooms are bright fuchsia red with a typical heavy damask fragrance. The flowers are similar in growth and bloom to Rose du Roi.

32

Rosa Paulii

Classed as a ground cover rose, dating prior to 1903, this rose flowers repeatedly.

The clean, light-green foliage provides a hardy, thorny barrier and functions as a ground cover for banks and hillsides. It produces strong shoots that eventually lie flat, with successive shoots creating a mound 2 to 3 feet high.

Rosa paulii flowers are distinctive. The bright white petal flares, standing apart from the others, creating flowers 4 inches wide with highly showy stamens in the centers. The blooms are clusters of 6 to 8 that follow each other in sequence. They have a nicely spicy fragrance.

Rosa Rugosa Rubra

This age-old rugosa flowers repeatedly and grows up to 5 feet tall.

No date can be found in tracing this rose's earliest history. It has fine attributes nevertheless. Plants are disease resistant, have a neatly arching habit—more so than most rugosas—and the 3 to 3½ inch flowers have five petals of rose wine coloration in the form of a star, with creamy stamens. Orange rose hips follow when petals fall, eventually providing their own display in late summer and fall.

Rose du Roi

This Rose of the King is an autumn damask, circa 1815, that flowers repeatedly on 3 to 4 foot compact plants.

From this noble ancestry the hybrid perpetuals have been developed. This variety sprang from breeding of original Portland roses and is one of the most hardy varieties that bloom from early spring to frost.

The rich, bright red of the central petals curls to reveal lighter red tones on the reverse. The outer petals seem almost blackish. Of course, it emits the traditional intense damask aroma.

Roseraie de l'Hay

This hybrid rugosa rose, dating to

1901, flowers repeatedly and grows between 4 and 6 feet tall.

Some authorities still debate whether this is a hybrid or pure oldtime rugosa, but its sparse crop of rose hips tends to prove it a hybrid. This large plant grows well as a luxuriant hedge, with dense foliage covering the entire bush. The long, pointed buds are deep fuchsia red, opening to display double 4-inch flowers of deep crimson, usually shaded with purple tones and bearing cream stamens. Its fragrance is deep and somewhat clovelike.

Rosette Delizy

This old tea rose, from 1922, grows 3 to 5 feet tall and flowers repeatedly. One of the most vigorous tea roses, it has the added advantage of being disease and also rather insect resistant. The compact flowers stand erect, producing well-formed flowers with cadmium yellow edging shaded with chestnut red. Many admirers find this an especially delightful old tea rose that outperforms modern hybrids, which require so much extra care. As with all tea roses, it has its special tea rose fragrance. Rosette Delizy prefers warmer climates and, in general, is too tender for northern gardens.

Rubrifolia

R. rubrifolia, dating from 1830, matures to 5 to 6 feet tall and flowers repeatedly.

The red canes on this hardy plant are attractive themselves, and the plants are especially sturdy across the country. Buds open to show warm pink, single blooms with well-defined stamens. These roses set bountiful and beautiful crops of rose hips each fall.

Rugosa Magnifica

An old oldtime rugosa, this flowers repeatedly and matures to 4 to 5 feet high.

A spreading plant with the glossy, ribbed foliage common to all rugosa roses, it is worth growing everywhere: It is sturdy, very hardy, and offers carmine-colored double blooms with strong, almost heady perfume. A real bee-attracting variety, as are most rugosas, this sets mounds of orange-red hips during the season.

34

Ruskin

Salet

This hybrid rugosa from 1928 grows 4 to 5 feet tall and flowers repeatedly.

According to rose scholars, this variety resulted from crossing a bright red hybrid rugosa and a red hybrid perpetual. The plants are quite hardy and develop well in northern areas. Flowers are brilliant red and double, formed in clusters on the vigorously growing plants. For its hardiness and performance, this oldtimer is well deserving of its popularity.

This moss rose, circa 1854, flowers repeatedly and matures to 3 to 4 feet tall.

According to its admirers, Salet performs as abundantly and consistently as a modern floribunda. Well-mossed, flared sepals cover beautifully formed pink buds. These open into lovely blooms with many tiny, closely packed petals. The perfume, of course, is the typical musk aroma of moss roses.

Sombreuil

Safrano

This tea rose from 1839 grows 3 to 4 feet tall and flowers repeatedly.

You can often find Safrano in gardens of historical homes in the Southwest, many up to 6 feet tall. The blooms are between fawn and apricot, and the fragrance is almost a blend of peaches and apricots according to its devotees. This tea rose prefers a warm, sunny spot and it is best grown only in mild climates.

A climbing tea among the oldtimers, Sombreuil, dating from 1856, flowers repeatedly on plants 5 to 10 feet tall.

Although, like most oldtime teas, this is too tender for most northern areas, it is deservedly popular in southern climates. The larger outer petals form well-proportioned buds that open like a cup, revealing many small, delicate petals of rich, creamy color.

Souvenir de la Malmaison

This Bourbon rose, circa 1843, grows 2 to 4 feet tall and flowers repeatedly.

The delicate outer petals of the tiny, perfect buds open to reveal a hundred or more small, fragrant, furled petals of the palest pink. It is obvious on examining this rose that there is tea rose in its heritage. Because of this, it is not hardy in cold climates. In warm ones, you will get profusions of flesh pink flowers, delightfully perfumed.

Oldtime Climbing Roses

Climbing American Beauty

This repeatedly flowering old favorite dates its heritage to just after the turn of the century, probably about 1909–10. It climbs 12 to 14 feet and bears large, fragrant flowers, cupped in form, on long stems that resemble those of its fabled parent, the American Beauty rose of the Gay Nineties.

This climbing rose is a strong, upright plant and is most suitable as a pillar rose, as well as one trained to trellis or fence. Once established, it produces an abundance of blooms for cutting as well as for exciting displays on the plant from the blooms remaining and being formed constantly.

Climbing Cecile Bruner

A climbing polyantha of 1894,

this rose grows or climbs 12 to 20 feet.

Unlike many other climbers, old and new, Cecile Bruner not only grows well in many areas, it bears abundant blooms in spring and continues to delight the eye into summer as well. Blooms are a lovely pink hue.

Climbing Columbia

From 1923, this climbing hybrid tea matures to 10 to 15 feet long.

This fine old climber with its rather strong growing habit has competed well for years with modern climbing roses. Its rose pink and sweetly perfumed blossoms are delightful, in true tea tradition. Unfortunately, this has become quite rare and difficult to find among old rose specialists today.

Climbing Lady Forteviot

Another climbing hybrid tea, developed in 1935, this grows 10 to 15 feet tall.

Fairly hardy, this climber has done well in many sections of the country. It offers very glossy, large foliage with dark green leaves touched with bronze. The flowers

that literally cover these climbing bushes are large and range from yellow gold to almost orange, with high centers. They are double and pleasantly fragrant.

Climbing La France

A climbing hybrid tea from 1893, Climbing La France grows 8 to 10 feet tall.

Developed from the bush La France hybrid tea rose, this delight is almost identical to its parent except, of course, in its growing habit. If you like La France, you can enjoy the beauty of this climber. Its blooms are pale pink very double fragrant flowers. Rosarians agree that when pruned back to stockier shape, it makes a magnificent, prolific shrub rose bearing blooms from bottom to top.

Climbing Shot Silk

This climbing hybrid tea from 1931 ranges between 10 and 15 feet.

With rather longer than usual stems and shoots, this double, fragrant rose has been limited in supply from nurseries in recent years. The high-centered blooms are cherry cerise shot with gold, giving an

37

appearance of coral pink. Among climbing hybrid teas, it offers most strikingly colored blooms on good stems for cut flower displays.

Felicite et Perpetue

A glorious rambler dating to 1827, this rose grows 8 to 10 feet. Its small, smooth leaves provide excellent foliage on a fence or wall. Clusters of buds are lightly touched with crimson. They open to flat, milk-white flowers with many tiny petals, and are delicately perfumed. Advocates of this rose say it produces a dazzling display on arbor or trellis.

Agnes

This hybrid rugosa dates back to the turn of the century and grows from 4 to 6 feet tall. It has one annual flowering, which is usually rather profuse. Occasional blooms may appear later during the season.

Agnes is reputedly the offspring of two hardy roses, one a rugosa and the other Persian Yellow. From this parentage, it too is completely winter hardy. The intense, dark green foliage is somewhat ribbed and provides a splendid background for the buds and blooms. This rose has fully double, nearly 3-inch flowers, which are a pale moon yellow. They cover the arching canes and have a sweet aroma with a tang to the scent.

Austrian Copper

This bicolor *R. foetida* traces its

heritage to the 1890s. It grows between 4 and 5 feet tall and has one annual flowering.

Although it flowers only once, the flowering is early. The 1-inch, single, brilliantly colored blooms are bright orange on the upper side of the petals, yellow on the bottom side, and they literally cover the plant. You will notice that after flowers are spent, petals drop, leaving the attractive gold stamens for a time. Austrian Copper does well in southern areas, but huge old plants have continued to thrive as far north as Wisconsin and Minnesota, attesting to its winter hardiness and vigor.

Belle de Crecy

This gallica rose was known prior to 1848 and produces one flowering per year on the 4-foot-tall plants.

One of the most fragrant of the old roses, Belle de Crecy bears 3 to 4 inch flowers, which are open and flat with many petals and a green eye at the center of each bloom. The newly opened blooms have cerise pink petals shaded with violet above and silvery blue violet below. As blooms fully open, the outer petals change to blue violet.

Despite its flowering but once a season, the fragrance for many is reward enough.

Belle of Portugal

This hybrid gigantea from 1903 will grow 20 to 30 feet long, but has only one annual flowering. It is popular in California and southern areas where it thrives with little care. Rapid growing, Belle of Portugal can climb tall trellises and into trees or up high walls. The long canes are covered with long, pointed buds, and 4 to 6 inch flesh pink flowers cover the plant during its month of bloom.

Unfortunately, despite its beauty and rapidly climbing growth, this rose thrives best only where winters are mild.

Carmaieux

A gallica rose originated in 1830, this annual flowering plant grows 3 to 5 feet tall.

On the plant, you'll enjoy large, fairly double blooms that are perhaps the most distinctly striped of any rose. The blooms themselves are white to blush pink with stripes of rose that turn slowly to violet and mauve shades. This lovely old rose performs well as a full-blooming specimen shrub.

Centifolia Muscosa Alba

A moss rose from 1810 or thereabouts, this annual flowering rose grows 4 to 5 feet tall.

Experts state that this is a white sport of the lovely Common Moss. Others refer to it as White Bath, Clifton Moss, or Shailer's White moss rose.

Its admirers note its strong perfume and its long, delicate, and intricate sepals. The petals have an almost tissue paper quality about them. This rose is in limited supply among old rose propagators.

Charles de Mills

It has been impossible to trace the forebears of this ancient French rose to establish a heritage date. The rose grows 4 to 5 feet tall and has one annual flowering.

As a bush or shrub, an established plant may be as much as 5 feet tall and 4 feet in diameter. In southern areas, it begins blooming in May and for the next 4 weeks or so can produce hundreds of 4-inch blooms. Petals are deep rose pink but you may see deep purple to lavender shades that whirl and swirl with the petals, exposing the silvery lavender on the reverse side of the petals. This rose is noted for its strong, heady rose perfume.

Common Moss

Rosa centifolia muscosa was known and loved prior to 1730. It grows 4 to 7 feet tall and flowers once annually.

Many rosarians consider this the most exquisite moss rose. It has long sepals almost like lace that flare out beyond the fully opened 2½ to 3 inch clear pink blooms. With delightful fragrance, this rose has retained its popularity for years and remains one of the most cherished of old-fashioned roses.

De Meaux

A *centifolia* type known before the 1700s, this annual flowering rose, which grows 2 to 3 feet tall, is ideal for beds and borders.

Tiny buds, as small as a lady's fingertip, open to reveal hundreds of pale to increasingly deep red petals. When fully open, flowers are about 1 inch across and have an intense fragrance.

This delightfully delicate little rose offers profusions of buds and blooms for displays and is worth cultivating despite its short annual flowering habit.

Dupontii

A shrub rose, dating from before 1817, this 7-foot-tall rose flowers once annually.

According to legend, this rose was raised by M. Dupont, who collected roses for the gardens of Empress Josephine at Malmaison. The beautiful shrub with blue-green foliage bears clusters of single, milk white to blush pink flowers all along its canes. The sweet fragrance is fruit-like, and the plant is nearly thornless. Despite its long history, this rose has become somewhat of a rarity.

Eglantine

This ancient sweetbrier traces its ancestry into lost pages of history. It flowers annually on 10 to 14 foot tall bushes.

In colder climates the plant remains more compact. In warmer areas, Eglantine nearly reaches the height of some climbing roses. It bears deep pink, single flowers for about a month in the spring. These are followed by large bunches of distinctively orange hips in the fall, adding color to the plants in that season.

Fantin-Latour

This 1850 *centifolia* rose flowers annually and grows on plants 4 to 5 feet tall.

Some authorities believe that this is the rose depicted in the painting "Roses in a Bowl" by the famed French artist for which it is named. The compact bush has large, smooth, dark green leaves. Blooms are typical *centifolia* with many pale pink petals that deepen to a warm blush at the center. The perfume from this old rose is arresting.

Father Hugo's Rose (Hugonis)

The *Rosa hugonis*, known since 1899, grows 4 to 6 feet tall and flowers once annually. It is also called simply Hugonis or the Golden Rose of China.

This delightful, graceful rose was discovered growing wild in China and brought into rose culture circles in 1899. Its arching branches with small leaves are so delicate that they remind one of maidenhair ferns. This is one of the first roses to bloom. It has small, cupped, bright yellow single flowers all along its branches. After blooming, the shrub grows new canes, which are red and covered with red prickles, adding to its appeal. The fruit hips look much like currants.

Felicite Parmentier

Flowering once each year, this alba rose grows 4 to 5 feet tall. Gray-green foliage on this fairly large plant is distinctive. It bears sizable pale pink flowers from 3 to 5 inches across. Blooms open with a swirl of many small petals which reflex to create a 2-inch ball with a green eye at the center. The perfume is delicate and pleasingly penetrating as it wafts across the garden.

Koenigin von Daenemarck

Also called the Queen of Denmark, this Alba from 1809 grows 4 to 5 feet tall and flowers once annually.

Blue-green foliage contrasts nicely with the clear white blooms. Flowers are 2½ to 3 inches across with good-sized outer petals of pink and quartered centers of small glowing pink petals. They are intensely perfumed. Under good culture a plant can produce many dozens of blooms at one time.

Lawrence Johnston

This hybrid *R. foetida*, originated in 1923, flowers intermittently on plants 6 to 12 feet tall.

Its great canes are covered with large, semidouble blooms of sunshine yellow through spring. Blooms are fragrant too. You also will be rewarded with occasional blooms later in the season. This extremely hardy rose grows upright and is self-supporting as a shrub or functions as a climber. The spent blooms neatly drop their petals, so other blooms are seen to fullest advantage.

Madame Hardy

This damask rose from 1832 grows 4 to 6 feet tall and flowers once annually.

With dark-green foliage, it is a sturdy bush bearing tight buds that have beautifully flared sepals through all stages. When fully open, the large, very double, flat white flower has a pronounced green spot on the center. Blooms are borne in clusters; the central buds are first to open in a pink flush that changes quickly to pure white. This too is intensely perfumed and is widely appreciated for its exquisite flowers as well.

Maiden's Blush

This alba rose flowers once annually on plants that reach 4 to 6 feet high. Its heritage has not been suitably traced.

With its unique blue-green foliage, Maiden's Blush offers a touch of pink to rose on new canes and thorns. It bears the palest blush pink in buds and flowers that deepen in color at the center of the bloom. Sepals are long, flared, and serrated. Legend says this rose is named for the Virgin Mary.

Petite de Hollande

This *centifolia* has one annual flowering on 4 to 5 foot plants. Its lineage traces back into lost history.

From the Greek era, *centifolia* roses were noted as the most fragrant in the world, and their many-petaled blooming habit has made them popular ever since. This rose bears clusters of 5 to 6 blooms from tight buds with long, flared sepals. The wide-open miniature flowers have large outer clear pink, highly scented petals circling many closely packed small ones around a green-eye center. An excellent rose for cutting for old-fashioned bouquet displays.

Rosa Damascena Trigintipetala

Developed prior to 1850, this rose stands 5 to 6 feet tall and flowers once annually.

Significant historically, this oldtime rose offers semidouble, deep rose-red blooms with showy stamens and is quite fragrant. Over the years, rosarians have debated among themselves about the differences between this rose and *Rosa gallica officinalis. R. gallica officinalis.* produces semidouble, fragrant, light crimson blossoms. However, it is a lower growing shrub that matures only to about 4 feet. It dates its ancestry before 1300. Both deserve places in old-fashioned rose gardens.

Striped Moss

Dating from 1826, this moss rose grows 3 to 5 feet tall, but flowers only once annually.

From its new green leaves tinged with red to its red prickles and sepals covered with red moss, the foliage itself is striking. Fragrant 1½ to 3 inch flowers open flat to reveal surprisingly striped petals. This unique moss rose ranges from candy-striped bright crimson and white to deep rose pink and pale pink stripes, depending on the weather. One fortunate additional attribute is that one stem with its several buds and flowers can be cut for a perfectly natural and lovely bouquet all by itself.

Tuscany Superb

This *gallica*, developed prior to 1848, grows 3 to 4 feet tall and has one annual flowering.

From this sturdy plant with its neat, dark foliage and almost thornless stems, you will enjoy superb blooms. The flowers are large, flat, and full of petals which are especially rich in their depth of color; almost blackish crimson and velvety yellow stamens grace the center and their fragrance fills the air around them.

Variegata di Bologna

This Bourbon rose of 1909, which grows from 5 to 8 feet tall, has one annual flowering but may offer a few chance blooms in early fall.

You can train this striking beauty on a trellis to admire its most unusual coloration and profusion of blooms. You'll see plump buds in clusters from 3 to 5 inches that open to become large, cupped, very double white flowers. Remarkably, they are graced with well-defined stripes of dark magenta to purple, a most pleasing appearance, especially when a fence is covered with hundreds of blooms from a display of several bushes.

Other Desirable Oldtime Roses

Dainty Bess

This hybrid tea, circa 1925, grows 3 to 4 feet tall.

One of the earlier hybrid teas developed, this oldtime classic has much to commend it. The long slim buds open to become 4-inch flowers of a dusky pink with 5 broad petals and showy maroon stamens. This variety is especially long lasting, both in the garden and as cut flowers for display in your home or at rose exhibitions.

Gruss an Aachen

This delightful floribunda, circa 1909, grows 2 to 3 feet high.

For 70 years this floribunda has performed spectacularly in gardens across America. The strong, spreading plant has rich green and glossy foliage with a bronzy hue. It produces nicely shaped buds of lovely shell pink color, and its flowers are a delightful shell pink. The blooms have large outer petals in cupped form which hold many furled and curled smaller petals within their cup.

Gruss an Coburg

Another hybrid tea developed in 1927, this matures to 3 to 4 feet.

From the early hybrid breeding programs, this strong, vigorously growing plant with its distinctive bronzy foliage has kept much of its popularity. The buds are a coppery pink that become double, fragrant, open flowers, with pale apricot— yellow petals. The reverse side of these petals remains the color of the unopened buds—a handsome sight for those who prefer this distinctive color in roses.

La France

Dating from 1867, this early hybrid tea has graced gardens here and abroad on its sturdy 3-foot bush.

Judged to be the first rose named "hybrid tea," this oldtime rose is well rooted in rose history. The pale pink buds open into delightfully large, very double flowers noted for their intense fragrance. It is one of the early ancestors of today's dazzling array of hybrid tea roses.

Madame Butterfly

A hybrid tea developed in 1918, Madame Butterfly grows 3 to 3½ feet tall.

From its famed parent Ophelia, this sport offers rather sturdy growth in hot and cold weather. The blooms are very pale pink to white, often combined with shadings of cream and pale yellow. In warmer weather, it tends to color somewhat differently, providing shades of pink and apricot in its blooms. As a hybrid tea, it has a notable perfume as well, but is becoming more difficult to obtain.

Margaret Ann Baxter

A hybrid tea, circa 1927, this plant grows 3 to 4 feet tall.

One of the most exciting and beautiful white hybrid tea roses according to some of its admirers, Margaret Ann Baxter is one of the more robust, healthy tea roses. Its foliage is somewhat leathery in appearance, but it produces such magnificent blooms you may find 70 to 100 petals in one of the large white blossoms. Some are slightly flesh colored at the center, and the scent is typically hybrid tea.

Marytje Cazant

From 1927, this polyantha grows 2½ to nearly 4 feet tall.

A bountifully blooming beauty, Marytje Cazant bears large clusters of tiny coral pink, waxy blooms. It is profuse in blooming habit and its flowers are long lasting. Many growers favor this for making corsages and the more delicate of old-fashioned rose bouquets.

Ophelia

A hybrid tea from 1912, this grows 3 to 3½ feet tall. From its beginning, many have favored this strong growing rose, unusual for a hybrid tea. It offers a delicate coloring of flesh pink with satiny sheen on its handsome bushes. It has a delicate aroma and, despite being difficult to obtain, provides another oldtime addition to rose tradition.

Orange Triumph

A polyantha from 1937, this grows 3 to 4 feet tall.

Because of its strong, upright growth and the perpetual blooms from this plant, you can enjoy its attraction in a garden or as a hedge, and plant it as a property border for glorious displays. The brilliant scarlet sprays of double flowers are only 1½ inches across, but the profusion of bloom throughout the season makes it a popular oldtime favorite for many. Despite its name, the flowers are scarlet, not really orange colored.

Perle d'Or

A polyantha from 1884, this plant grows 3 feet high.

From years back, this early polyantha has healthy foliage that resists mildew and diseases as well as rose insects. Perle d'Or deserves a place in more gardens. The sturdy plants bear delicate miniature roses of pearly, pink gold color. It is also called Yellow Cecile Brunner by some admirers because they feel its amber-flesh pink more aptly earns that name.

Souvenir de Madame Boullet

A hybrid tea, circa 1921, Souvenir de Madame Boullet grows 2½ to 3½ feet tall.

· This vigorous plant tends to spread well and produces many large, well-formed blossoms. Those who grow it favor it for its almost amber and moonlight tones. It also has the traditional fragrance of hybrid tea roses.

White Pet

A polyantha circa 1879, White Pet grows 2 to 2½ feet tall.

This low-growing rose fits perfectly into beds and borders. Favored for its resistance to mildew and pests, this hardy little polyantha performs beautifully. The blooms open from clusters of perfectly formed tiny buds and are a delicate blush pink that turn whiter as they become fully open. Good for garden display and cutting as well, a mature plant has enough blooms to look like a giant snowball in summer.

3
Rose-Planting Review

Planting is no mystery to rose lovers. However, since we all tend to take shortcuts at times, perhaps it is best periodically to review the basic, proven steps, to be certain we get our old-fashioned roses rooted right.

Roses, fortunately, are surprisingly hardy and capable of good growth for years, providing they get that proper root-hold initially and are given reasonable care through their years in our gardens. Here's a down-to-earth good-growing review of rose planting basics.

First point to consider is the individual plant. Reputable rose growers, especially those that specialize in old-fashioned varieties, work hard to produce the best quality plants for your garden. Every quality rose is a handmade product. There is no way to bud and graft on an assembly line. Yet every year too many people hunt for bargains.

The echoes of one advertising campaign still linger, although the plants it sold are long since dead. The radio commercials said simply, "These are not just number one roses, they are not number two or number three roses either. They are number four roses and only $4.95." Thousands of people sent in their money to buy the spindly, weak, barely alive number four rosebushes.

Dig a hole that will accommodate the rosebush roots when they are spread adequately. Place the plant on a mound of soil in the hole.

Firmly tamp soil around roots to eliminate all air pockets.

Then tamp soil firmly with your foot.

Slowly pour water (from half a bucket to a full bucket) around the newly planted rose and let it drain away.

Mound the soil 6 to 8 inches around newly planted bush.

As a person who knows and loves roses, you are no doubt aware of the time and effort that is spent to graft buds of desired rose varieties on the sturdy wild-rose root stocks.

Growers then cut off the top of the wild rose so all the strength of the vigorous root system goes directly into the new stem. A single stem is not enough, of course. A number one plant must have a minimum of three healthy stems. Rose nursery growers must prune the grafted plants until they produce these additional healthy, strong stems. About the end of the second year, sometimes the third, the plant is ready for sale to rose enthusiasts.

These efforts are hand efforts, done with care to ensure that the delicate process of budding roses produces the desired strongly growing, healthy, and sturdy plants you want and deserve. Considering the work that has been lavished on producing duplicates of the fine old-fashioned roses you desire, it pays to take that little extra time and attention to plant them right.

Your rose garden's location should give your roses at least a half day's full sun. Roses like the sun, but don't favor being baked by blazing sun too long each day. Soil should be loose and friable, so pick a well-drained area. While it is true that roses prefer lots of water, it's also true that they don't like wet feet. Soggy soil and areas that contain large amounts of clay should be avoided. You can, of course, improve such areas by incorporating generous amounts of peat moss or finished compost into the soil and even adding sand to loosen heavy soils. Where possible, select sites with natural sandy loam soils.

To the best natural soil, you should add and mix in 25 percent by volume of peat moss and, where available, 15 percent by volume of well-rotted manure or compost into the rose bed itself.

Plan and prepare your planting area well before the roses you have ordered arrive. Before planting them, unpack the bushes and soak their roots in water 12 to 24 hours. This helps soften the roots so they can begin to send out feeding root hairs as soon as you have planted them.

Dig a hole about 18 inches deep and mound soil in the center so that the roots may be spread apart without crowding. The graft union, that knob where the new rose was budded onto the wild variety, should be at ground level in temperate climates. It should be just below soil level in cold areas and slightly above ground level in subtropical regions. Some old rose varieties may not be grafted of course, if you prefer the oldtime wild rose. These should be planted as deep as they grew in the nursery. You can usually see the soil line on the stem, just above the point where the roots begin to form and branch.

Cover the roots with your improved soil mixture. A combination of equal parts soil, peat moss, and compost or well-rotted old manure is excellent. Carefully work and pack this soil mixture around the roots with a blunt stick or your fingers and fist. Be sure to prod and firm the soil to eliminate all air pockets in the soil.

Fill the hole two-thirds full of this good soil mixture. Then, use your foot to tramp the soil firmly around the roots. Now add water—a bucketful or at least a half bucketful. This too helps settle the soil and eliminates hidden air pockets underground. When the water has drained away, finish filling the remainder of the hole with soil and tamp it lightly.

After planting, mound remaining soil 6 to 8 inches high around your newly planted bushes when planting in either spring or fall. This prevents drying of tops until roots have taken hold. Remove this mound of soil when all danger of freezing is past and after the new growth begins in spring.

Many types of fertilizer products are available to nourish your roses. The fact is, specialized rose foods have been developed that are designed specifically to give roses the best possible nourishment. Whichever brand you buy, always follow the label directions exactly. With fertilizer, as with pesticides, a little goes a long way. Too much can sometimes be as damaging as too little or none.

Other rose books can provide more detailed instructions on rose planting and care. Since this book about old-fashioned roses is designed for those who already know most of the preferred rose care methods, only a refresher on planting basics is included here.

4
Plantscape with Roses

If you enjoy old-fashioned roses, it follows naturally that you'll want to put them on permanent display to enjoy their beauty around your home grounds. Since a picture often is worth much more than mere words, especially to suggest ways in which you can plant and enjoy the magnificence of roses, this chapter will guide you to rose plantscaping.

Naturally, you can mix and match roses with a variety of other flowers and shrubs around your home grounds. In my *Plan Your Own Landscape* book, many different displays for homes of all types are included.

In this book you'll find a variety of illustrations. The illustrations include combinations of modern roses from hybrid teas, floribunda, grandiflora, and climbing roses to old-fashioned types that grow together gloriously. These fine and often innovative suggestions have been gathered here through the courtesy of a veteran rose grower and a friend, George Rose, of the All America Rose Selections. For many years, he has been responsible for encouraging millions of people into the dazzling and fragrant world of rose gardening. He has also been the guiding light behind the creative and worthwhile campaign that saw 1979 become the Year of the Rose across America.

You can use roses to your heart's desire, wherever you live and garden. If you wish them on a porch or patio, balcony or rooftop garden in a city, you can have your wish come true. Combination growing mediums of humus and peat moss are readily available today to fill tubs, planters, raised beds, and other decorative containers for your rose gardens.

If you wish to pursue your rose growing fever even further, most likely you will wish to ally yourself with others in the American Rose Society. Thousands of rose enthusiasts like yourself share both their common and uncommon interests in roses through this fine nonprofit association. The membership card is your passport to rose shows, rose gardens, and rose fellowships everywhere. That includes the 118-acre American Rose Center in Shreveport, Louisiana, headquarters of the American Rose Society, and the largest park in the United States devoted primarily to roses.

Members also receive a colorful monthly magazine with timely articles and useful information for growing, showing, and enjoying roses. The *American Rose Annual*, a 220-page book with beautiful color illustrations and rose information plus descriptive lists of roses, is one of the members' benefits. And, through membership, members may request advice on problems related to rose growing anywhere. This service gives you access to fellow rosarians throughout the country, experts who share their love and knowledge of a wide variety of old and new roses. There's even a group within the society that is dedicated and devoted to old-fashioned roses.

There are also more than 350 local chapters and affiliated societies of the American Rose Society, all dedicated to learning and sharing rose-growing experiences. The Society's address is Box 30,000, Shreveport, Louisiana 71130.

As you look ahead to more glorious horizons in your own rose gardens, consider these ideas and the variations that can apply in your own environment.

My thanks to the All America Rose Selections for all the illustrations in this chapter.

Tree and bush roses combine naturally along a driveway and entrance walk.

Roses grace a doorstep, a lovely welcome to your home.

Roses are effective in a dooryard garden bed.

Try roses in raised or sunken beds on your patio.

Rose gardens border two sides of this garden sitting area.

Enjoy a curve of roses in a corner of border.

Climbing roses add beauty to your dooryard fence.

Roses used in this way make a living garden hedge.

Climbers combine tastefully with a privacy screen.

An effective place for roses is beside a patio entrance.

Here's one way to have roses right on your terrace.

Consider roses for use around your entrance porch.

You can add the color of roses in front of evergreen border.

Roses mix well in flower borders.

In a city garden, roses provide welcome color and fragrance.

A child's garden of roses is a treat.

Try roses around a birdbath or sundial.

You can plan for roses just about anywhere you'd like them.

Roses add a touch of grace at a garden gate.

5
Culture and Care Review

Since so much has been written in profuse detail about rose care already, this book is primarily directed to those who wish to dig into the increasingly popular field of old-fashioned roses. I have assumed that you already are well rooted in rose care and culture.

However, it is perhaps appropriate to include a brief review of this subject. These generally hardier and less disease susceptible roses have won new popularity today for their ability to thrive with less care than many of the newer hybrids. Nevertheless, it always pays to retrace the growing steps that can assure fullest success with roses of all types.

Location   It is not vitally important whether plants receive morning or afternoon sunlight. They must receive, however, at least a half day of sun. Partial shade actually is preferable to a full day of sunlight for most roses.

Soil should be reasonably loose and friable, and by mixing in peat moss and compost as indicated in the brief review on planting, you can improve rose growing conditions. Tree roots have a nasty habit of interfering with rose growth. They invade underground, of course, and can quickly rob rose plants of moisture and nutrients. Avoid tree root areas if possible when you select your rose bed locale. If tree roots are present, you can dig a trench around the bed as deep as tree roots extend. This cuts off all roots that might enter the bed to interfere with your rose plants' growth. Refill the trench with soil after digging and severing roots and you should eliminate the problem. It is, however, helpful to dig a trench around your bed every few years to intercept any new tree roots that might have wandered into it.

Best planting time is spring, when the soil is warmed and workable. You can plant container-grown roses in warmer weather, but most mail order nurseries from whom you obtain old-fashioned roses ship plants dormant and bare rooted. This requires spring planting in most cases. You can plant in fall if you can obtain plants from nurseries that ship in fall. But why forgo an entire season of blooming beauty to wait until fall for planting?

Soils Avoid both extremely heavy, clay soils and extremely light, sandy soils. In the first case, the soil will hold excess moisture and this can lead to rotted roots. Roses don't like wet feet. Sandy soils lose nutrients that leach away from the root feeding zone and also dry out too rapidly. You can improve heavy soils by adding peat moss, humus, and compost made of rotted organic matter. These materials also increase the water-holding capacity of sandy soils.

Planting Take the time to plant each rose right. Consult the step-by-step guide in this book as a reminder for proper and successful procedures, whatever time of year you elect to plant roses.

Feeding Many special rose foods are now available under a variety of brand names. Most experts agree that you should not feed newly set roses. However, established plants should be fed according to the label directions for whichever brand of rose food you use. Plants, like people, can be overfed. That can cause problems, from burning to forcing overly rapid growth. This is especially bad in the fall, because tender new growth is more susceptible to winter kill in cold areas.

You can sprinkle rose fertilizer, which is balanced to provide the right amounts of nitrogen for vegetation growth and phosphorus and potash (potassium) for root and bloom production, in several ways. Some rose growers prefer to scatter the fertilizer around the bushes, then scratch or rake it into the soil and water the area to help dissolve the fertilizer. Others prefer pellets that can be pressed into the ground. Others recommend punching holes in the circle around the bushes or plants and filling these with fertilizer, which then dissolves into the soil when watered or during rains.

Be sure you read and heed the label directions. Too much food is both wasteful and can overfeed your plants. Be sparing as you feed, rather than overgenerous. And do not feed your roses after September 15 in most areas, to avoid creating tender growth which will most likely be damaged in the winter.

Pruning and Care Planting and care of old and species roses are generally the same as for modern roses. Pruning, however, requires a somewhat different practice.

As a general rule, old-fashioned roses that bloom repeatedly should be pruned in the late winter or early spring before new growth begins. Old roses that flower once annually should be pruned only after they have bloomed in the spring.

It pays to study your individual old-fashioned roses so that you get to know their own particular habits and personalities. Some of the older varieties that bloom repeatedly should not be pruned except to remove weak or dead growth. Much of their continuing beauty lies in their ability to produce a large plant with hundreds of flowers. If you prune them too harshly, as you would modern hybrid tea or floribunda roses, you will not be rewarded with the desired mass of blooms.

To create a desired bushy, many-branched plant, shorten the long canes by one-third after the plant blooms. You should also shorten lateral canes a few inches. You may continue this judicious pruning practice until late summer, and from that point, leave the plant alone until after it blooms the following spring.

You may wish to be more designing with some of your old-style roses too. Pegging is the use of any method to bring the canes into an arched, horizontal, or other desired pattern or position. You may accomplish this by hooking an 8 to 10 gauge wire over a matured cane and securing it into the desired position by pushing the other end of the wire into the ground.

You may also tie the canes in an arched position to stakes or a trellis if you wish. This tying and training causes the flowering stems to grow all along the canes. Once you have two or three canes arched over and tied to stakes or trained in the position you wish them to grow, it is possible to weave other canes among them for a fuller, more abundant growth pattern.

You may, of course, fasten long canes to fences or similar supports. However, after two or three years, it is a good idea to remove a few old canes so that new ones will be stimulated to grow from the plant to replace the older, weaker ones.

Watering Best culture for roses, favored by many expert growers, is clean cultivation. If you follow this time-honored practice, you will seldom need extra watering. Others, more veteran growers, however, prefer to use a light mulch of peat moss or wood chips, which also provides a natural look as well as helps retain soil moisture.

Many parts of our country have experienced droughts of varying lengths during the past decade. Some droughts have been severe and prolonged. If your area doesn't receive adequate rainfall every week or two during the growing season, irrigation will be needed to ensure continued adequate rose growth. Soak the ground thoroughly for several hours to be certain that water penetrates well into the root zone. Frequent light waterings only encourage surface weeds. Water in the morning, never the evening. This avoids problems of fungus diseases which can form on wet leaves, especially in warm weather.

Mulching, of course, helps retain soil moisture. It also helps keep soil cooler in hot weather, and the old mulch can be scratched into the soil of established beds to improve them each spring before more is added for appearance. One final thought. Hold off on water in the fall, as with fertilizing, to avoid forcing tender new stem growth which will be susceptible to winter injury. Roses naturally begin their dormant period from September to November, depending on the climate in which they grow.

Disease and Pest Control Most of the old-fashioned roses have a natural tendency to resist diseases. That has been one of the reasons for their reborn popularity, in addition to their graceful and often more delicate appearance. However, diseases may arrive. A little attention can avoid the problem.

An ounce of prevention surely is worth the effort. Most rose growers feel that dusting is preferable to spraying, because it is easier and quicker. If you have a combination of old and new roses, a pest prevention program makes good sense.

Powdery mildew and black spot are two of the most insidious rose diseases. By treating plants on a regular weekly or twice monthly dusting or spraying schedule, you avoid problems.

Insects are rather easily controlled. Diseases, on the other hand, can be harder to conquer if they do become established. Fortunately, modern products arm you with effective ways to control these perennial problems. Here's a brief, close look at these problems and what is currently recommended for control.

On young leaves, powdery mildew first appears as slightly raised blisterlike areas that soon become covered with a grayish-white powdery growth. As the young leaves expand, they become curled and distorted. On older leaves, large white patches of the fungus appear but there is very little distortion. Affected buds become covered with the white mildew before they can open and either fail to open or open improperly. Infection often spreads to mature flowers, causing flower blight.

As the name black spot implies, the most common symptom of this disease is black spots on the leaves. Several other diseases also cause dark spots on the leaves, but you can distinguish black spot by the dark color and the infringed border of the spots. At times, chlorosis, the distinctive yellowing of the green parts of the plant, may also be detected around the lesions. Black spot causes premature leaf drop and may result in severe defoliation of the plant. Continuous attack causes unattractive plant foliage as well as reduced size, number, and quality of blooms.

Black spot usually occurs on the lower portion of the plant first. High humidity and intermittent wet leaf surfaces' favor growth of the fungus. Although roses may vary in susceptibility to black spot, no variety is completely immune. Hybrid teas are generally more susceptible than other varieties.

Following a regular spray program will help control black spot and powdery mildew. Start spraying as leaf buds are forming and continue throughout the growing season. Acti-done, Benlate, and Karathane will control powdery mildew. Apply according to label recommendation. Apply Acti-done and Karathane only at temperatures of 85° F. or lower; application at temperatures higher than 85° F. will burn the leaves. Benlate can be used at any temperature.

Black spot can be controlled by applying a dormant spray of lime sulfur, 1 part chemical to 15 parts water, just after pruning in autumn and spring. Applications of other fungicides are also necessary to control black spot. You can get excellent control with either Benlate, Maneb, Daconil 2787, or Zineb. Make applications every 7 to 10 days, particularly during rainy periods. Apply Benlate at 14 to 16 day intervals. You may want to mix fungicides or alternate them throughout the growing season. Also, most fungicides can be mixed in spray tanks with insecticides. Combination products make application easier.

Keep roses well mulched throughout the season. Plants that receive too much or too little water are more susceptible to diseases than well-watered plants. Collect and burn fallen leaves in autumn and spring. Carefully collect and destroy infected buds and leaves. Be sure to prune all diseased canes.

Pests, too—mites, aphids, thrips, beetles, slugs, and other assorted insects—can, from time to time, invade your rose beds and bushes. Again, it is better to be prepared and protected than to try to battle the bugs once they begin their onslaught or become established.

Garden centers provide a wide range of pesticide materials. Combination insecticide-fungicides are the best bet. They control a wider range of insect and disease problems and can be applied in one dusting or spraying on an established schedule. Specially formulated rose pesticides are your best bet.

As with fertilizer, a word of caution is in order. Pesticides are designed to control disease and kill insects. Apply only as label directions indicate. Too much can burn foliage and injure plants and is wasteful as well.

Winterizing In southern areas, mounding soil or mulching heavily around rose bushes is seldom necessary. In more northern areas, you may wish to follow one of several procedures, from mounding soil 6 inches to 12 inches around the plants in late fall, to covering with straw, and even untying and covering climbers. It is best to check with local rose growers on the winterizing procedures that work best in your own locale. There's no need to do extra work if it isn't necessary. Besides, many local gardeners have found ingenious ways to protect their plants that you can adopt yourself.

6
Lasting Elegance Indoors

Your old-fashioned roses can be elegant as cut flowers indoors too. Here are ways to be sure that they last longer, whether you wish just a few in a simple vase or prefer to use them in more formal arrangements.

You'll find a detailed checklist at the end of this section. First, however, consider some of the facts of life that can contribute to longer vase life of cut roses. Much of this information is based on research done by Dr. H. Paul Rasmussen of the Department of Horticulture at Michigan State University.

When you cut a rose from your plant, remember that you sever it from its own life support system. As soon as that cut is made, the rose is like an astronaut without a life support system, and it is in trouble. Before you cut the rose, it had obtained all the components for life from the plant.

The components of a life support system for the cut rose, which it obtained from the plant before being removed, are nutrients, sugar, cool temperatures, antiaging compounds, and most important, water. All these ingredients are dependent on a continuous and ample supply of water since they are all soluble or carried into the rose in water.

Research has revealed that a molecule of water can move from the base of a 24-inch cut rose to the petals in 30 seconds or less. Such movement occurs when the cut rose is in the light at room temperature. The cells in the stem of a rose, which carry the water, are like a handful of soda straws.

As long as straws are in a glass of water, you can draw water up through them. Take them out of the water while sucking on the straw and you draw up only air. Keep that fact in mind when you work with cut roses.

The rose stem does the same thing because its demand for water is continuous, even when severed from the mother plant. The big difference, however, is that the cells in the rose stem have end plates or small screens that allow water to pass but block the passage of air. A small bubble of air is formed and trapped at the end of the rose stem when it is cut from the plant. When the base of the stem is blocked with air, more water cannot get up the stem, even if you replace that stem in water. In effect, the rose is very near its life support system, the water, but cannot get to it.

Another interesting phenomenon that shortens vase life occurs when a rose is removed from the plant, and sugars which move from the leaves down to the root continue to flow for a short time. When the flower is cut from the plant, the sugars have no place to go. These sugars can move across the cut surface of the stem and be drawn up into the water-conducting cells where they can crystallize or become solid and thereby also block the water-conducting cells. This is especially true if air has moved into these cells first.

In the case of air or sugar blockage, or a combination of both, the life-giving supply of water is cut off or reduced and the rose will wilt and die, even if replaced in water. Fortunately, both air and sugar blockage of the rose stem are restricted to the first one-half inch of the stem where you made the base cut. You can solve this problem simply by recutting the base of the stem to remove the blockage and give the rose a chance to be rehooked to its life support water system in the vase. The process is simple, but you must pay attention to its basics. To avoid letting the base of the stem gulp in another air bubble and block it when the new cut is made, place the stem end under water in a container or under running water in a sink. That ensures a water supply to the rose. Then, when you recut the stem, a small droplet of water hangs on the cut end so you can safely move the stem to the vase with water where you plan to display your handsome blooms. Always keep this cut end moist.

Occasionally a rose will wilt or develop a weak stem just below the bud, causing the bloom, especially a heavy one, to tip over. If you simply remove that bloom from the arrangement, recut a one-inch section from the base of the stem under water, then submerge the entire bloom, stem, and foliage for twenty minutes or so, you'll discover that the flower revives nicely and can be replaced in the vase or your arrangement. When you attempt reviving a cut rose this way, be sure the water is about 100°F. and that you straighten the angle of the head. If you don't, it will revive with a bent neck.

Flower food also contributes to longer life of your cut flowers. You can increase vase life of roses 30 to 50 percent if you use floral preservative or flower food, as it is often called. Mix this material in the vase of water according to packet or label directions.

When you display roses indoors, remember that sudden or extreme changes in the environment also will shorten vase or display life. Don't place cut roses in direct sunlight, in front of a radiator or air-conditioning outlet, or in a very warm room. Cut roses don't like a lot of heat, and they can't stand drafts.

With this understanding of proper care for longer and more elegant life from cut roses, here's a brief checklist of how to keep your roses appealing.

Remove any leaves that might decay under water in the container. This may sound obvious, but it is one important step that is often overlooked.

While holding the stem end under running water after you have brought the rose indoors, cut about one inch of stem off each rose with a sharp knife or shears. This opens up the water conveying layers of the stem so the cut flower can absorb water more rapidly. When removing leaves or thorns, be certain you do not cut through the bark, or scrape the bark. This avoids leaving a damaged area where bacteria can enter.

Place roses in a clean, deep vase of warm, not cold or cool water. Warm water is more readily absorbed and won't shock your cut flowers. If possible, leave the cut roses in a cool room or a refrigerator to condition them for two to four hours before beginning your arrangement.

To prolong the life of your cut roses even further, add a good floral preservative to the water. As with plant feeding and pesticide use, mix only the exact amount recommended on the label. A little does the job properly; too much is harmful.

If you prefer to use florist's porous foam for making arrangements, follow these tips. Saturate the foam thoroughly in advance in clean water containing a floral preservative. Most foams should not be reused since they may harbor harmful bacteria from former bouquet or arrangement water. Use a large enough vase to permit complete submerging of the block or section of foam. If you don't submerge it, this material can act like a wick to evaporate water from the container.

Be sure that the stem ends of all cut roses are below the surface of the water, and add sufficient water daily to replace that which is used by the flowers. You may be surprised how rapidly cut flowers take up the water you originally provided.

After inserting the rose stem, do not remove it. This avoids leaving an air pocket at the base of the stem which can lessen that stem's ability to draw up the water it needs to stay fresh.

Attention to these simple steps will let you enjoy your old-fashioned cut roses longer in your home.

7
Rose Display Gardens

All across America in 1979, gardeners and rose enthusiasts alike celebrated the Year of the Rose. It is safe to say that this coast-to-coast observation resulted in the planting of millions more roses, modern hybrids as well as more old-fashioned roses.

Traveling the country while writing this book, we've talked with hundreds of rose growers. Many tell us that there is a new feeling for nostalgia shared by many oldtime rose growers and novices alike. As a consequence, old-fashioned roses too are gaining popularity.

As you travel on vacation or to see what's new in gardens around your area, there are many places that welcome you to enjoy magnificent rose displays.

So that you may enjoy your rose gardening pleasure even more, plan to visit some of these public gardens. The list in this chapter gives all the public rose gardens we have found in our research. Some are at colleges and universities; others are in state and city parks; still others are part of large botanical gardens.

When you visit, ask about your favorite roses. The expert gardeners who planned and planted these public rose gardens are especially happy to share their rose-growing secrets with you.

WASHINGTON, D.C.
Shoreham Hotel Rose Garden
2500 Calvert St., N.W.

CALIFORNIA
Arcadia Co. Park Rose Garden
Corner Campus Dr., Holly
Ave. and Huntington Drive,
Arcadia
Berkeley Municipal Rose Garden
Euclid at Bay View Pl.,
Berkeley
Fresno Municipal Rose Garden,
Roeding Park
890 W. Belmont, Fresno
Descanso Gardens
1418 Descanso Drive, La Canada
Exposition Park Rose Garden
701 State Dr., Exposition Park
Los Angeles
Morcum Amphitheatre of Roses
Jean St. off Grand Ave., Oakland
Fairmont Park Rose Garden
NW corner Redwood Drive &
Dexter Ave., Riverside
Capitol Park Rose Garden
13th & "L" Sts., Sacramento
Golden Gate Park Rose Garden
Golden Gate Park, San
Francisco
San Jose Municipal Rose
Garden
Naglee & Diana, San Jose
Huntington Botanical Gardens
1151 Oxford Road, San
Marino

City Rose Garden
Los Olivos & Laguna Sts.
Santa Barbara
Memorial Rose Garden
Armory Grounds, 700 E.
Canon
Perdido St., Santa Barbara
Visalia Garden Club Public
Rose Gardens
Tulare Co. Courthouse,
Visalia
Westminster Civic Center Rose
Garden
8200 Westminster Ave.,
Westminster
Pageant of Roses Garden
Rose Hills Memorial Park
3900 So. Workman Mill Road
Whittier

COLORADO
Longmont Memorial Rose
Garden
Roosevelt Park
7th & Coffman, Longmont

CONNECTICUT
Norwich Memorial Rose Garden
200 Rockwell St., Norwich
Hamilton Park Rose Garden
Plank Road, Waterbury
Elizabeth Park Rose Garden
915 Prospect Ave., West
Hartford

FLORIDA
Cypress Gardens
Cypress Gardens, Florida

GEORGIA

Greater Atlanta Rose Garden
  Greenhouse Area
  Piedmont Park, Atlanta
Thomasville Rose Test Garden
  1840 Smith Avenue,
  Thomasville

HAWAII

University of Hawaii College of
Tropical Agriculture
  HAES, Maui Branch, Kula

IDAHO

Memorial Bridge Rose Garden
  N&S Highway, Lewiston

ILLINOIS

Grant Park Rose Garden
  Between Balboa & Jackson-
  Chicago
Marquette Park Rose Garden
  3540 W. 71st St., Chicago
Gardener's Memorial Garden
  1707 St. John's Avenue
  Highland Park
Cook Memorial Rose Garden
  413 N. Milwaukee Ave.
  Libertyville
Peoria Park District Rose
  Garden
  Glen Oak Park Conservatory
  2602 Prospect Road, Peoria
Robert R. McCormick Memorial
  Gardens
  Cantigny, Roosevelt &
  Winfield Roads
  Wheaton

INDIANA

Lakeside Rose Garden
  Lakeside Park
1500 Lake Ave., Ft. Wayne
  E. G. Hill Memorial Rose
  Gardens
  Glen Miller Park, Richmond

IOWA

Iowa State University Rose
  Garden, Ames
Bettendorf Community Center
  Rose Garden
  2204 Grant St., Bettendorf
Huston Park Rose Garden
  3d Ave. & 15th St. SE
  Cedar Rapids
VanderVeer Park Municipal
  Rose Garden
  236 W. Central Park Avenue
  Davenport
Greenwood Park Municipal
  Rose Garden
  4812 Grand Ave., Des
  Moines
Inter-State Nurseries Rose
  Garden
  2201 Washington St.,
  Hamburg
Weed Park Memorial Rose
  Garden
  Muscatine
Mount Arbor Demonstration
  Garden
  Shenandoah
Iowa Rose Society Garden
  State Center

Byrnes Park Memorial Rose
Garden
Orange Grove & Campbell
Ave., Waterloo

KANSAS
Kansas State University Rose
Garden
Dept. of Horticulture
Waters Hall, K.S.U.,
Manhattan
E.F.A. Reinisch Rose & Test
Gardens
Gage Park, Rose Drive,
Topeka

LOUISIANA
L.S.U. Rose Test Garden
137 Agronomy—Hort. Hall,
L.S.U., Baton Rouge
Pauline Worthington Memorial
Rose Garden
City Park, New Orleans

MASSACHUSETTS
The Stanley Park of Westfield,
Inc.
333 Western Ave., Westfield

MICHIGAN
Michigan State Univ.
Horticulture Gardens
East Lansing
Frances Park Memorial Rose
Garden
3200 Moores River Dr.,
Lansing

MINNESOTA
Duluth Rose Garden
13th Ave. E. & London Road
Duluth
Minneapolis Municipal Rose
Garden
Roseway Road & Lake
Harriet Blvd.
Minneapolis

MISSOURI
Cape Girardeau Rose Display
Garden
Perry Ave & Parkview Drive
Cape Girardeau
Blue Ridge Mall Rose Garden
Jackson County Rose Society
I. 70 & U.S. 40 at Blue Ridge
Blvd.
Kansas City
Laura Conyers Smith Memorial
Rose Garden
5200 Pennsylvania Street
Loose Park, Kansas City
Missouri Botanical Rose Garden
2315 Tower Grove Avenue
St. Louis

MONTANA
Missoula Memorial Rose Garden
Sunset Park
Brooks & Mount Sts.,
Missoula

NEBRASKA
Lincoln Municipal Rose Garden
Antelope Park, 2740 "A" St.
Lincoln

Omaha Memorial Park Rose
  Garden
  56th & Underwood, Omaha

NEVADA
Reno Municipal Rose Garden
  Cowan Drive
  Idlewild Park, Reno

NEW JERSEY
Brookdale Park Rose Garden
  Bloomfield
Colonial Park Rose Garden
  Mettler's Road, East Millstone

NEW MEXICO
Prospect Park Rose Garden
  8205 Apache Ave., N.E.
  Albuquerque
Community Rose Garden
  Lea General Hospital
  1701 North Turner, Hobbs

NEW YORK
Cranford Memorial Rose
  Garden
Brooklyn Botanic Garden
  Brooklyn
Niagara Frontier Trail Rose
  Garden
  Humboldt Park, Buffalo
Queens Botanical Garden
  43-50 Main St., Flushing
The National Rose Garden
  1111 South Main St., Newark
United Nations Rose Garden
  United Nations, New York

Maplewood Rose Garden
  100 Maplewood Park Ave.
  Rochester
Central Park Rose Garden
  Central Park, Schenectady
Sterling Forest Gardens
  Tuxedo

NORTH CAROLINA
Raleigh Municipal Rose Garden
  Pogue St., Raleigh

OHIO
Columbus Park of Roses
  4015 Olentangy Blvd.,
  Columbus
Ohio State University Rose
  Garden
  2120 Fyffe Road, Columbus
Kingwood Center
  900 Park Ave., West,
  Mansfield

OKLAHOMA
J.E. Conard Municipal Rose
  Garden
  Honor Heights Park,
  Muskegee
Municipal Rose Garden
  Will Rogers Park
  3500 N.W. 36th St.,
  Oklahoma City
Tulsa Municipal Rose Garden
Woodard Park
  2435 So. Peoria Avenue,
  Tulsa

OREGON

Corvallis Municipal Rose
  Garden
Avery Park, Corvallis
George E. Owen Municipal
  Rose Garden
  100 N. Jefferson St., Eugene
International Rose Test Garden
  400 S.W. Kingston Ave.,
  Portland

PENNSYLVANIA

Malcolm W. Gross Memorial
  Rose Garden
  2700 Parkway Blvd.,
  Allentown
Hershey Rose Gardens &
  Arboretum, Hershey
Longwood Gardens, Inc.
  Kennett Square
Renziehausen Park Arboretum
  Renziehausen Park
  Eden Park Blvd., McKeesport
Reading Municipal Rose Garden
  505 South 12th St., Reading
Penn State University Rose
  Garden
  University Park, State College
The Robert Pyle Memorial Rose
  Garden
  West Grove

SOUTH CAROLINA

Edisto Rose Garden
Edisto Memorial Gardens
  U.S. 301 South, Orangebury

TENNESSEE

Municipal Rose Garden
  Warner Park, Chattanooga
Memphis Municipal Rose
  Garden
  Audubon Park, Memphis

TEXAS

Corpus Christi Rose Society
  Display Garden
  Louisiana Parkway & Hewitt
  Dr. at Santa Fe
  Corpus Christi
Samuell-Grand Municipal Rose
  Garden
  6200 East Grand, Dallas
El Paso Municipal Rose Garden
  Copia at Aurora, El Paso
Ft. Worth Botanic Garden
3220 Botanic Garden Drive
  Ft. Worth
Houston Municipal Rose
  Garden
  1500 Hermann Drive,
  Houston
Municipal Rose Garden
  Civic League Park
W. Beauregard & Park St.
  San Angelo
Tyler Rose Garden Park
  1800 West Front St., Tyler

UTAH

Territorial Statehouse Rose
  Garden
  Old Capitol State Park,
  Fillmore

Municipal Memorial Rose
  Garden
  1st North 1st East, Nephi
Salt Lake Municipal Rose
  Garden
  1050 E.S. Temple, Salt Lake
  City

VIRGINIA
Arlington Memorial Rose
  Garden
  Wilson Blvd. and Lexington
  St. North
  Arlington
Mountain View (Fishburn)
  Garden
  714 13th St., S.W., Roanoke

WASHINGTON
Fairhaven Park Rose Garden
  108 Chuckanut Drive,
  Bellingham

Chehalis Municipal Rose
  Garden
  Chehalis
Woodland Park Rose Garden
  700 N. 50th St., Seattle
Rose Hill—Manito Park
  West 4 - 21st Ave., Spokane
Point Defiance Park Rose
  Garden
  5402 N. Shirley, Tacoma

WEST VIRGINIA
Ritter Park Rose Garden
  McCoy Road, Huntington

WISCONSIN
Boerner Botanical Garden—
  Whitnall Park
  5879 South 92 St., Hales
  Corners

You can also learn more about roses through participation in the courses and activities of leading botanical gardens. They welcome members and offer tremendous programs in all of the horticultural areas to their membership, including magnificent rose gardens and training courses in the planting and pruning, care and culture of roses.

Some that come to mind are the New York Botanical Garden at Bronx, NY 10458, which has the very beautiful Edwin De J. Becktel Memorial Rose Garden; the Brooklyn Botanical Garden, 1000 Washington Ave., Brooklyn, NY 11225, which has the very fine Cranford Memorial Rose Garden, with Peter Malins as rosarian. He is one of the finest rosarians in the country. At Flushing, New York, is the Queens Botanical Garden, 43-50 Main Street, which has a rose garden of about 4,000 plants.

There are, of course, hundreds of local rose societies all over the country, but most of them are tied in with the national American Rose Society. The various garden clubs of America are interested in roses, along with all other plants, but their interest in roses, of course, is only of a general nature.

8
Rose Test and Comparison Gardens

As one of the most popular flowers across America, roses are on display in many public gardens. New roses, hybridized from the sturdy, hardy old favorites, are constantly being tested and compared with the long-time favorites. You may wish to visit some of these All-America Selections display gardens.

This list is arranged by states, followed by Canada and foreign countries, where thousands of roses can be seen and evaluated, new with older ones.

AK Agr. Exp. Station
Dr. Donald H. Dinkel
University of Alaska
College, AK 99701

Family Food Garden
Mr. George Wells
P.O. Box 1014
Grass Valley, CA 95945

L.A. State & Co. Arboretum
Mr. John W. Provine, Supt.
301 N. Baldwin Ave., Box 688
Arcadia, CA 91005

Strybing Arboretum
Mr. John Bryan, Dir.
9th & Lincoln Way
San Francisco, CA 94122

Cal. Poly. State Univ.
Mr. David Focht, Supt.
Dept. of Horticulture
San Luis Obispo, CA 93407

Hort. Arts Society of CO.
  Springs
P.O. Box 9812
Colorado Springs, CO 80932

Denver Botanical Gardens
Mr. Glenn Park
909 York St.
Denver, CO 80206

Dept. of Hort. (PERC)
Dr. Ken L. Goldsberry
CO. State University
Fort Collins, CO 80525

Walt Disney World Co.
Mr. Ron Gindlesperger
P.O. Box 40
Lake Buena Vista, FL 32830

Orange County Ag. Center
Mr. Thomas MacCubbin
Extension Agent III
2350 E. Michigan Ave.
Orlando, FL 32806

Univ. of Hawaii
Ag. Exp. Station
Mr. Phillip E. Parvin, Supt.
Maui Br., P.O. Box 197
Kula, HI 96790

Rockome Gardens
Mr. Roger Kirkwood
Route 2
Arcola, IL 61910

Dept. of Hort., Ext. Serv.
Prof. A.E. Cott
Iowa State Univ.
Ames, IA 50011

Eldora Training School
Mr. John E. Matusch
Eldora, IA

Dept. of Hort., L.S.U.
Prof. Claude S. Blackwell
Baton Rouge, LA 70803

Hodges Gardens
Mr. Rodney Sharpe, Horticul-
ture
P.O. Box 921
Many, LA 71449

Brookside Gardens
Mr. Robert Haehle
1500 Glenallan Ave.
Wheaton, MD 20902

Michigan State University
Dr. William Carlson
The College of Agric. and Natu-
ral Sci.
Department of Horticulture
East Lansing, MI 48823
AND
Prof. Milton Baron, L.A.
310 Manly Miles Bldg.
East Lansing, MI 48823

Dow Gardens
Mr. Doug Chapman
1018 West Main St.
Midland, MI 48640

Hidden Lake Gardens
Dr. Fred W. Freeman
Cur. & Assoc. Prof.
Tipton, MI 49287

Wayne County Ext. Dir.
Donald D. Juchartz
5455 Wayne Road, P.O. Box 550
Wayne (Detroit), MI 48184

Minneapolis Park Board
Mr. John Lanns
250 South 4th St.
Minneapolis, MN 55415

Univ. of MO., Dept. of Hort.
Dr. R.R. Rothenberger
1-43 Agr. Bldg.
Columbia, MO 65201

Botanical Garden
Jackson State College
Prof. Peter Lane, Dir.
Jackson, MS 39217

Flower & Garden Test Grounds
c/o Miss Rachel Snyder
4251 Penn. Ave.
Kansas City, MO 64111

MO Botanical Garden
Mr. R.J. Dingwall, Ch. Hort.
2345 Tower Grove Ave.
St. Louis, MO 63110

Univ. of New Hampshire
Mr. Charles H. Williams
Plant Science Dept.
Durham, NH 03824

Thompson Park
Mr. John Hoffman
Asst. Supt. of Parks
P.O. Box 326
Lincroft, NJ 07738

Morris County Park Comm.
Mr. Quentin C. Schlieder
Dir. of Hort.
53 Hanover Ave.
Morristown, NJ 07960

Cook College, Rutgers U.
Mr. Malcolm R. Harrison
Ext. Specialist in Floriculture

AND

Dr. William O. Drinkwater
Specialist-Vegetable Crops
Blake Hall, Box 231
New Brunswick, NJ 08903

Skylands Gardens
Mr. Hans E. Bussink
Box 1304
Ringwood State Park
Ringwood, NJ 07456

NMS Univ., Dept. of Hort.
Dr. Fred B. Widmoyer, Head
Box 3530
Las Cruces, NM 88003

Queens Bot. Garden Soc., Inc.
Mr. Roland G. Wade
43-50 Main St.
Flushing, NY 11355

Sterling Forest Gardens
Mr. M. Colborne, Mgr. of Hort.
Box 608
Tuxedo, NY 10987

NC State Univ., Hort. Dept.
Prof. Joseph W. Love
Kilgore Hall
Raleigh, NC 27607

City Board of Park Comm.
Mr. Frederick L. Payne
950 Eden Park Drive
Cincinnati, OH 45202

Kingwood Center
Mr. Frederick E. Roberts, Dir.
P.O. Box 966
Mansfield, OH 44901

Longwood Gardens
Dr. Russell J. Seibert, Dir.
Kennett Square, PA 19348

Peddlers Village
Mr. Earl Jamison
Lahaska, PA 18931

Univ. of R.I.
Prof. Walter Larmie
Plant & Soil Science Dept.
Kingston, RI 02881

Clemson Univ. Hort. Dept.
Dr. A.J. Pertuit, Jr.
Clemson, SC 29631

Univ. of Tenn., Dept of Hort.
Dr. G.L. McDaniel
Box 1071
Knoxville, TN 37901

Dallas Garden Center
c/o Mr. Joe M. Woodard
8636 Sans Souci Drive
Dallas, TX 75238

Univ. of Vermont
Dr. S.C. Wiggans, Chmn.
Dept. of Plant & Soil Sci.
Burlington, VT 05401

Kings Dominion
Mr. Roy G. Rector
P.O. Box 166
Ashland, VA 23005

Norfolk Botanical Gardens
Mr. G.W. Baker, Curator
Airport Road
Norfolk, VA 23518

Busch Gardens
Mr. William C. Shelburne, Jr.
P.O. Drawer F.C.
Williamsburg, VA 23185

Univ. of Alberta
Dr. E. W. Toop
Plant Science Dept.
Edmonton, Alberta
    T6G 2E3 CANADA

Assiniboine Park
Mr. M. J. Hebert
2355 Corydon Ave.
Winnipeg, Manitoba
R3P OR5, CANADA

Borough of Etobicoke
Mr. A. J. Higgs, Parks Supt.
Civic Centre
Etobicoke, Ontario
M9C 2Y2, CANADA

University of Guelph
Mr. I. L. Nonnecke, Chmn.
Dept. of Hort. Science
Guelph, Ontario
N1G 2W1, CANADA

Royal Botanical Gardens
Mr. George Pagowski
Box 399
Hamilton, Ontario
L8N 3H8, CANADA

Ornamental Research Serv. Bld.
50
Mr. George D. McDiarmid
Agriculture Canada
Ottawa, Ontario
K1A OC6, CANADA

Board of Parks & Rec.
Mr. L. A. Wright, Supt.
Sarnia City Hall
Sarnia, Ontario, CANADA

Metropolitan Toronto Parks
Dept.
Mr. Thomas W. Thompson,
Comm.

12th Flr., Phoenix House
439 University Ave.
Toronto, Ontario
M5G1X8, CANADA

Ontario Hort. Research Inst.
Mr. B. Hamersma
Vineland Station, Ontario
LOR 2E0, CANADA

Bermuda Botanical Gardens
Mr. Gordon R. Groves, O.B.E.,
Dir.
Box 834
Paget East, BERMUDA

Hurst Gunson Cooper Taber
Ltd.
Mr. Ralph Gould
Hurst No. 2 Breeding Grounds,
Feering
Colchester, Essex, ENGLAND
C05 9NL

Tres Rios Jardín
Sr. Oscar Brauer Herrera, Jefe
Culiocán, Sinaloa, MEXICO

Wellington City Parks & Re-
serves
Mr. Ian Galloway, Dir.
Town Hall
Wellington, NEW ZEALAND

Parks, Recreation & Beaches
Mr. T.A. Linley, Dept. Dir.
P.O. Box 3740
Durban 4000, SOUTH AF-
RICA

9
Sources of Oldtime Roses

You may find sources for those lovely old-fashioned and sometimes rare roses right in your own neighborhood, or through friends who also share your love of these delightful roses. More likely, you'll need to extend your search across the continent.

Here are some of the sources for old-fashioned roses. Some offer free catalogs and a few may charge for their colorful illustrated catalogs. A few don't sell mail order, but perhaps a special letter from a rose devotee like yourself will lead to good relations and a chance to purchase a few select roses.

WESTERN NURSERIES

1. Bush Nursery (no mail order or catalog)
   8501 S. Lone Elder
   Canby, OR 97013

2. Roseway Nurseries (free catalog)
   2935 Southwest 234th Ave.
   Beaverton, OR 97005

3. Stanek's Garden Center (free catalog)
   E. 2929 27th Ave.
   Spokane, WA 99203

4. Stocking Rose Nursery (free catalog)
   785 N. Capitol Ave.
   San Jose, CA 95133

5. Tillotson's Roses (catalog with order)
   Roses of Yesterday and Today
   802 Brown's Valley Road
   Watsonville, CA 95076

6. United Rose Growers (price list)
   1531 Guild Road
   Woodland, WA 98674

EASTERN NURSERIES

7. Earl Ferris Nursery (free catalog)
   Hampton, IA 50441

8. Joseph J. Kern Rose Nursery (no catalog)
   Box 33
   Mentor, OH 44060

9. Palette Gardens (catalog 50 cents)
   20 W. Zion Hill Road
   Quakertown, PA 18951

10. Thomasville Nurseries, Inc. (free catalog)
    Box 7
    Thomasville, GA 31792

11. Wayside Gardens (catalog $1)
    Hodges, SC 29695

12. Wyant's Roses (free catalog)
    Route 84, Johnney Cake Ridge
    Mentor, OH 44060

CANADIAN NURSERIES

13. Caro Pallek & Son Nurseries (free catalog)
    Box 137
    Virgio, Ontario

14. Pickering Nurseries (free catalog)
    670 Kingston Road
    Pickering, Ontario

Old-fashioned roses may be difficult to find. Those in this book are usually available from one or more of the nurseries and suppliers listed here.

If the roses you desire are not available commercially, you have an option. You can write to one of the people indicated here who are deeply rooted themselves in Heritage Rose history and activities, enclosing a self-addressed, stamped envelope for reply. They may be able to guide you to a source of cuttings or budwood for propagating. These Heritage Rose Coordinators are:

- *Northeast:* Lilly Shohan, RD1, Clinton Corners, NY 12514.
- *Northcentral:* Henry Najat, MD, Rt. 3, Monroe, WI 53566.
- *Northwest:* Jerry Fellman, 947 Broughton Way, Woodburn, OR 97071
  Edith C. Schurr, 1123 Fifth Ave. South #2, Edmonds, WA 98020.
- *Southwest:* Miriam Wilkins, 925 Galvin Dr. El Cerrito, CA 94530.
- *Southcentral:* Vickie Jackson, 122 Bragg St., New Orleans, LA 70124.
- *Southeast:* Doris Simpson, 200 Ridgemede Rd., Baltimore, MD 21210.

Index

Pasture rose, 5, 7-8
Paul Neyron, 16, 31
Pax, 16, 31
Penelope, 16, 31
Penzance sweet brier, 6
Perle d'Or, 17, 47
Pest control, *see* Disease and pest control
Petite de Hollande, 17, 43
Planting review, 51-55; digging the hole, 54-55; fertilizer products, 55; first point to consider, 51; sun and soil considerations, 54, 55
Plantscape, 57-60
Powdery mildew disease, 76-78
Prairie rose, 8
Prickly rose, 7
Prince Camille de Rohan, 16, 31-32
Pruning and caring, 75-76

Rasmussen, Dr. H. Paul, 81
Reines des Violettes, 16, 32
Roger Lambelin, 16, 32
Rosa Canina, 14
Rosa Damascena Bifera, 16, 32
Rosa Damascena Trigintipetala, 17, 43
Rosa Paulii, 16, 33
Rosa de Rescht, 16, 32
Rosa Rugosa Rubra, 16, 33
Rosaceae family, 3-4
Rose, George, 59
Rose hip teas, 4
Rose petals, 4
Rose du Roi, 16, 33
Roseraie de l'Hay, 16, 34
Roses: background and heritage, 3-9; Christian symbolism, xiv-xv; culture and care of, 71-78; display gardens (All-American Selections), 95-101; indoor cut flowers, 79-84; introduction to, xiii-xv; list of display gardens, 85-93; in mythology, xiv; planting review, 51-55; plantscape, 57-60; sources for, 105-107; species available, 11-48
Rosett Delizy, 16, 34
Rubrifolia, 16, 34
Rugosa Magnifica, 16, 34
Rugosa rose, 5, 6, 8
Ruskin, 16, 35

Safrano, 16, 35
Salet, 16, 35
Scotch rose, 5, 7
Sombreuil, 16, 35-36
Souvenir de Madame Boullet, 17, 47
Souvenir de la Malmaison, 16, 36
Striped Moss, 17, 43-44
Sweet brier (or eglantine) rose, 5, 7, 16, 41

Tea rose, 5, 6-7, 8, 14
Trigintipetala, 17, 43
Tuscany Superb, 17, 44

Variegata di Bologna, 17, 45

Watering, 76
White Pet, 17, 47-48
Wild roses, 7-9
Winterizing, 78

Year of the Rose (1979), 59

Zineb (fungicide), 78